OUT OF MY ASHES, I WILL RISE!

Wanda D. Kidd

Out Of My Ashes, I Will Rise!
by Wanda D. Kidd

Printed in the United States of America

ISBN 978-1-60791-692-5

www.xulonpress.com

DEDICATION

This book is dedicated to the memory of my dad, Clarence "Chink" Jackson." Dad was a loving man who taught us unwavering faith and love. He loved and adored God, and every aspect of his life demonstrated that love. He was a man who showed his family that you pray, not only for your friends, but for your enemies as well, and you will be blessed. He took the Word of God at face value and did not want to be found guilty of disobedience to any part. He always said that he wanted to be able to preach freely from Genesis to Revelation, and he did.

Dad always taught us to avoid saying, "I can't," but instead when facing challenges in life to remember that *"I can do all things through Christ which strengtheneth me" (Phil. 4:13).* He was also a great family man! He showed us God through abundant love, laughter, fun, and enjoying God's creation in various family venues. He showed us God through faith and obedience to the Word, which in turn was demonstrated through the manifestation of great blessings and abundant favor in his life as well as ours. We are grateful to have been blessed with such a special man in our lives. To us, he is the epitome of Christ's light and shining example. He is the epitome of true love. I am grateful to have had such a gift in my life!

CONTENTS

INTRODUCTION

Imagine waking up one day only to find that you are in a place where there seems to be nothing else left to your life but ashes. Even after looking at the remains of the ashes, you realize that the only visible sign of your life is nothing more than the horrid fumes rising up from the pile. As you view the trail of smoke rising upward and smell the stench of what was, you experience a shocking jolt of reality and wonder where any evidence of your existence is. Your ashes are the results of the issues and battles that have confronted your life. Your ashes mark the losses you have experienced throughout your existence. They are a compilation of your hurts, betrayals, and disappointments. They culminate every experience designed to kill and destroy you.

Your ashes are supposed to signify your demise. They are a representation of the charred destruction of dreams and aspirations. Your ashes are a compilation of words from every tongue that spoke against your success and everyone who pronounced and applauded any failure. And even if there flows a breeze of hope to glide over your remains and to breathe life and escort you out of your pain, those ashes only seem to scatter briskly in the wind until there is nothing left, as a representation of all that could have been.

Ashes symbolize the loss of a loved one or the death of a relationship that you thought would last forever, the death of the hope that you once had, the death of your will to even survive. It represents the remains of a broken heart that houses the fragments of your life and shattered vision. What is significant about ashes is that they are remains. They do not look like anything specific, but just a reminder of hopelessness and despair. To you, there is nothing even recognizable to even spring forth hope.

Yet there is a remedy! If God can reach down and take dirt and form man, then breathe the breath of life for man to become a living soul, then He can breathe life into your lifeless situation. That one breath has multiplied and sustained humanity for centuries. Before God breathed the breath of life into man, He had to first see the value of man, the purpose of man, the life in man. He sees something of value still left in you!

God will take the remains of what you think is nothing more than ashes, what looks like nothing more than ashes, and breathe life into a dead situation. While you have been preparing for burial, God has been preparing for a celebration of life—*your life!*

If you give God the opportunity, He will cause life to flow through the veins of your existence and will raise you right up out of your ashes to where the ashes soon become a distant memory of what was supposed to kill you, what was supposed to hold you captive until you died. He will raise you up in authority and victory, and you will reign in abundant life—in every area of your life!

Throughout this reading, various spiritual principles are repeated in order to ensure that you thoroughly understand that you do have a choice. You can choose to remain where you are and stay a prisoner of your past, your pain, and disappointments or, on the other hand, you can choose to live! You can live the abundant life that you were ordained to live. *Choose life! "I call heaven and earth to record [witness] this day against you, that I have set before you life and death, blessing and cursing: therefore choose life that both thou* [you] *and thy* [your] *seed* [your children, grandchildren and generations to come] *may live"* (Deut. 30:19; also read Deut. 30:15–16).

CHAPTER 1

WHY THE PAIN?

When you find yourself with your back against the wall, what do you do? Some will stand and fight, and others will flee. Some will give in to the situation and to their feelings, while others will continuously cling onto hope with all that they have. It is always easy to say what you will or will not do when you are on the outside looking in. While your life is being lived in blissful delight, you can only stand on that side and anticipate how you would handle any given situation. However, when life's challenges submerge you in pain and you are found dripping with despair, you may begin to wonder, why the pain? You, no doubt, feel that there must be a reason why you are confronted with this situation that has brought so much heartache. And you, no doubt, wonder what the remedy is for becoming free from the chains that bind you in every situation that you face.

Everyone, at one time or another, experiences hurt or pain. The difference between success or failure, agony or defeat, and stagnation or mobility is how you handle the pain. Your thinking can imprison you in the pain or release you to move forward in victory. There are some situations in life that just happen. Life just comes at you! Life itself will bring you its share of surprises. You can even go through life trying to dot every "i" and cross every "t," but you, too, will experience some pain. You may be able to assess your own choices and, hopefully, take responsibility for them. However, what about when you suffer because of the decisions of others? What can you do to become empowered?

You may regret some of the choices that you have made in life and are still carrying the scars from. You may ask God why it is that you made certain choices. Please understand that God does not tie your hands and force you to make the right decision. He can lead you, but you must be willing to be led. You may ask God why it is that you cautiously or prayerfully make certain choices in order to avoid certain unpleasant consequences, yet you still experienced pain because of the decisions of others. We all understand that in life you will get hurt sometimes. From some hurts, you certainly bounce back quickly. Then, other hurts penetrate your very being. Yet you made certain choices to avoid certain situations that would bring about critical hurts and pain. You did not want to experience the consequences that came with those choices. But, because you are not an island and relationships do come in and out of your life, you have found that you still have experienced great pain. But you do not have to stay there!

You may be one who wraps your pain in a blanket, gives it a pacifier, and provides it with nutrients; that is, pampers, cuddles, or woos it. When you provide nutrients to your pain, you will see it grow from infancy to the adult stage, which means expansion. You may even use excuses when your pain shows out and is evident in other areas of your life, your actions, or your character. You may use the excuse of pain and hurt for your actions toward others and even toward yourself. But yet within, you are not happy; you have not seen days of joy and fulfillment in a while; and your relationships are consistently broken because you have never been healed of the pain that you carry.

But now it is time to take off the blanket, throw away the pacifier and bottle, and stop pampering your pain. Stop toasting the enemy when he pulls you into failure and bondage. Move from victim to victor! But in order to understand pain, to understand how to move in pain, and finally to answer the question, "Why the pain?" you must understand certain spiritual concepts.

Understand that whether one is a believer or not, generally anyone can see the two forces working and moving in this world.

To sum it up, the movie producers often culminate their messages through film with good versus evil. In the general movie themes, you will always see a good character versus an evil character; you will always see a good situation versus a bad or evil situation. Throughout the movie, you will see the characters faced with situations in which they have to make choices. These choices will determine their success or failure, their happiness or sorrow, their victory or defeat. Sometimes the movie may not end the way that you thought it would end. Sometimes you may find that there is a surprise ending—something that you never expected to happen, happens.

Art does mimic life. In life, you have situations that will arise. You have choices to make while being challenged through various adversities. In life, there are times when you will see success and failure—victory and defeat. In life, there are surprises that may arise, those situations that you never expected to see or experience. It is at those times that you may wonder, why? I believe that if you are honest, you will see that some experiences came from your own wrong choices. Then, in other cases, they may have come through the wrong choices of others. In other cases, it was just the challenges of life. Regardless of how you got there, you just want to understand why the pain and grief surrounds you and how you can be set free.

Let us examine God's intent when man was created. In the book of Genesis, we can see that man was created in the image of God. Man had direct access to God. God provided man with everything that he needed: food, dominion, companionship, and spiritual leadership. God loved Adam so much that He created Eve by taking one of Adam's ribs and sculpting a vision of beauty. Then He presented *Eve* to Adam, as a Father presenting a bride to the groom. God provided man with *intellect* and told Adam to name all the animals. God provided man with *authority* and said that they (Adam and Even) were given *dominion* over every animal and every creeping thing. God gave man His best. But He also gave man a *command* that everything He had provided was for him; however, he was not to eat from the tree of the knowledge of good and evil (Gen. 2:17).

Here you have Adam and Eve's confrontation of *choice*. Why would God put a tree in direct view, yet give a command not to eat from it? I believe God wanted man to understand the importance of choice and obedience from the beginning. God told them that on the day they ate the fruit from this tree, they would surely die. Good and evil did exist, because God and Satan existed. (Even Satan had a choice). But obedience shielded Adam and Eve from the evil. Can you imagine if your only experience in life was to live in goodness, peace, and abundance? Obedience *shielded* man from eternal pain!

Now Satan saw that Adam and Eve had a place in God's heart. Satan used to have a well respected place in heaven until pride rose up and he tried to exalt himself against God (Isa. 14:12–16). He lost his place, and now he hated the fact that man has a special place in the heart of God. Man would now receive all the benefits of the kingdom. Therefore, Satan hated man. He hated God. So now he seized the opportunity to try to hurt God by destroying man. When Satan tempted Eve, she had a choice not to yield. She had a choice not to listen. She had a choice not to converse with him, but she did. Lend your ear to the enemy, and he will whisper words of death!

The Bible says that Eve listened to the subtle words of Satan and *"saw that the tree was good for food, and it was pleasant to the eyes, and a tree to be desired..."* (Genesis 3:6). She did eat of the fruit, in direct disobedience to God. Notice that after she ate the fruit, there was no action or judgment that occurred. Then she gave the fruit to Adam to taste, and he did. After he did eat, *"the eyes of them both were opened, and they knew that they were naked..."* (Genesis 3:7).

"Naked" refers not just to the physical aspect of exposure, but also to the spiritual aspect. They were now exposed and vulnerable to their flesh and to Satan. They were open and bare. They now became more vulnerable and susceptible to the dictates of the flesh and *sinful* desires. Their eyes now became open to sin and flesh.

Before Adam and Eve ate the fruit, they experienced desire, which is why Satan was able to entice them. He planted a seed by appealing to the appetite of the flesh for pleasure, as well as to their intellect with reason. Through their intellect, they reasoned that Satan's words had truth. Also, through the seductive words of Satan, their curiosity and desire were heightened until they succumbed to temptation. Yet, full exposure to the dictates of the flesh did not occur until they actually yielded and ate the fruit.

Adam and Eve had a choice but yielded to temptation. If they had not been capable of resisting, God would not have told them not to eat of the fruit. He would have known that they could not resist. Yet, He did know that they were capable of making the right choice, although they did not make the right choice. This is when pain began.

Adam and Eve were now exposed and became accessible to the knowledge of good and evil. This now meant struggles with sinful desires, as well as battles with intellect and reasoning versus the voice of God and faith. Satan had told Eve that God did not want her to eat of the fruit because they would become as *"gods, knowing good and evil."* (Genesis 3:5). Isn't it amazing how something that sounds as reasonable and harmless as eating a piece of fruit or making one wrong decision can create havoc in your life with an avalanche effect?

Certainly, now they did know good, evil, and the dictates of the flesh. *To know* is not only to have knowledge of but also to sometimes experience. Satan will take a truth and pervert it by hiding the ultimate consequences. The death that Adam and Eve experienced was not a physical death at that time, but a spiritual death. Their innocence was gone. Their relationship with God as they knew it was severed. They no longer even looked at themselves the way that God had designed them—in liberty and freedom. They had been guiltless, but now they were guilty. They had been free, but now they were in bondage.

When their eyes were opened, they ran and hid their nakedness. What had been created as beauty was now tainted. What had been created in perfection was now marred. Sin distorts all that is good and perfect in the sight of God. Sin is in direct opposition to what God wills for mankind.

When they heard the voice of the Lord, they hid themselves from the presence of God. Sin hates the presence of God! When God began to speak to Adam, He said, *"Who told you that you were naked? Have you eaten of the tree, whereof I commanded thee that thou shouldest not eat?"* (Gen. 3:11 AMP) This was a rhetorical question asked to Adam, since God already knew the answer.

Notice that God did not address Eve first after the sin, although she was the one who first ate the fruit. He called Adam. Why? It is because Adam was the spiritual covering, and he was given the command not to eat of the tree. In turn, Adam said, *"The woman that you gave to be with me - - she gave me [fruit] from the tree, and I ate"* (Gen. 3:12 AMP). Adam immediately transferred blame to Eve. He did not take accountability. (As a sidenote, this is also an example of how the enemy comes into marriages to separate today: by the avoidance of responsibility, transfer of blame and accountability, which results in dividing and conquering).

Anyway, God eventually addressed Eve afterward and asked, *"What did you do?"* Then Eve transferred some blame and responsibility to the serpent (Satan) and said, *"The serpent beguiled me, and I did eat"* (Gen. 3:13). Sin never wants you to face yourself and take responsibility for your own actions. Sin and flesh are always willing to blame someone else for their own ungodly actions. But I say to you today, it is a matter of *choice!*

Then the Lord pronounced judgment upon the serpent, Eve and Adam. Understand that you will reap the consequences of the seeds that you sow, the choices you make. Adam and Eve's choices brought spiritual separation between mankind and God. In addition, through their disobedience, they experienced their own pain when their son Cain murdered his brother Abel.

Sin destroys not only you, but it can also destroy your seed. Adam and Eve opened the door to sin in their family and to mankind. Satan is not just after you, but he is also after your seed! He is after your children, as well as your spiritual seed—the gifts, talents, and abilities that were placed inside of you. He is after the call that God has on your life. He is after you so that you will not fulfill your purpose and accomplish those things assigned to you—to reach those people assigned to your hands and also to walk in the richness planned for you. Disobedience to God will always cause pain, whether you are the one who is in direct disobedience to the will of God, or someone else in your life makes the wrong choices. It will always cause pain and severe consequences.

Adam and Eve's disobedience caused an avalanche of sin throughout mankind's existence, and if we look in this world, we can still see the consequences. We can still see and feel the pain that was ushered in by Adam and Eve's actions from years ago. But the wonderful thing about God's love is that He sent His Son, Jesus Christ, just to help you get through life's pain and so that you can still experience victory in your life and live above the curse of darkness.

The number one thing to remember is to stand on the Word of God in accordance with the will of God. It is the power of the Word that guarantees victory. But victory is often measured in different ways. There are those who feel that victory is achieved only when that which would come against them never manifests. In other words, when you do not have any problems, then you are victorious. If the weapon never forms, then you are victorious.

This, however, is not true. Some things God does allow, regardless of how the door was opened. Pain can be the very thing that God uses to launch you into a victorious place. You must understand that while you are here on this earth, there are some things that you have to go through. That is because you live in a sinful world.

We would love for it to be different now. We would love for everything to be wonderful at all times. But in this life, you will still experience some suffering. There is a definite battle in progress, good versus evil. And the pain that you experience is just a consequence of disobedience from centuries ago.

The good news and blessing is that as an individual you have the right to choose how you go through your challenges in life. You have the opportunity to live a victorious life through the Word of God. Remember, you were never meant to get comfortable in this world in its sinful state. But after Jesus came, died, defeated Satan, and resurrected with all power in His hands for our sins, you can now, once again, experience the true glory that God intended for mankind from the beginning—even here on this earth!

Although this world is filled with sin and degradation, you can still have peace and joy and experience true love and all the benefits of the kingdom of God. God may allow you to go through some things, but He can also take that very situation and use it to strengthen you, build your life, and work on your behalf. He can use it to open your eyes to a revelation knowledge that can cause your life to soar.

You are developed throughout your pain and suffering. You should learn compassion for others as well as obtain patience in suffering. It is a fact that many, through pain, seek God more. Now He has your full attention. Now you will hear Him more clearly. Your pain can cause you to walk in the purpose that God intended for your life.

No, it does not take pain all the time to get you to your destined place. However, if you are confronted with a challenge that brings pain to your life, God can seize the opportunity of your painful situation to show you just how wonderful He is. He can also use the situation to show you how powerful you are.

While in pain, it is a great opportunity to say, "Lord, flex Your muscles in my situation." It is an opportunity for God to show you another side of Himself. It is another chance for God to increase in your life. This is a chance for God to prune you and remove all those things that hinder your life, remove those people who were sent to destroy your life or bring distractions to your life, develop character and integrity, as well as add peace in your home and to your spirit man. So as a result of your pain, your trust in God can grow deeper, your love for God can grow deeper, and your faith in God can increase limitlessly.

Rest assured that there is an appointed day of deliverance for you! Victory is simply bringing you out so that God can get the glory. Others have gone through tragic situations, but from that situation, they pressed past their hurt to continue to live. They pressed past the initial shock and the questioning of why it happened. They moved forward in an attempt to reach out to survive, live and to help others.

Some organizations have been formed because of those who have gone through challenging and/or tragic events. Wonderful laws have been implemented because someone experienced a heart-wrenching trauma that was turned into an opportunity to help someone else and make a difference. There are ministries that have been birthed out of pain. Relationships have been revitalized because of pain. And lives of others have been saved because someone reached out beyond his or her own personal painful experiences to bring life to another.

When it is all said and done, your mind is the determining factor of whether you will stay in your pain and live beneath your privilege and God's will or whether you will walk in victorious living as God intended for you to do. Now I ask you, will you remain "there"—in that place of hurt and pain—or will you allow God to raise you up out of your ashes? The choice is *yours!*

CHAPTER 2

WHO CAN I TRUST?

W hen people have experienced acute pain and experienced feelings of betrayal and abandonment, it can cause them to raise walls of suspicion and build barriers of defense. It can leave them vulnerable.

One of the primary things that a wounded individual looks for is trust. Trust and safety go hand in hand. It is devastating to seek refuge and safety in the confidence of someone who appears open and understanding, someone who is willing to embrace you and understand your hurts, only to later find out that you opened yourself to someone who really wants to see you fail, someone who wants to see you fall. If this happens, you end up with only layers and layers of hurt and abuse, coupled with uncertainty and vulnerability and a spectrum of other inner struggles. The wounded person who has gone through a traumatic experience simply wants to know, "Who can I trust?"

Oftentimes these wounded souls venture out to find someone they can trust, someone who can understand their struggles. Oftentimes they find that the very ones they thought they could trust are the very ones who will turn on them in times of need. Countless times people may leave a devastating situation wounded and vulnerable and search for someone that they feel can help heal and help fill the void. They often turn to someone that they believe can help put them back together.

Sadly, this has backfired on countless occasions. First, it is up to the one who is wounded and hurt to embrace healing within first. If the heart is not healed and you are not made whole from the inside, you will never experience the fullness of life and will continue to be vulnerable prey to ruthless predators. Inevitably, there will always be aspects of your emotions that war with your mind or rehash the past, the pain and the agony.

Oftentimes people will try everything else, such as vices like drugs, alcohol, or sex, in order to ease the pain. These and other vices are simply bandages and deceptive devices to pull you further into bondage. What they do is merely mask the pain. They never confront the pain and deal with resolution of the pain. They never make you whole but continue to fragment your life. They can become addictive and ensure that the only escape from reality and pain is to indulge in these actions. Then, when the high is gone, when the temporary pleasure is over, the pain and reality of the pain still exists. This is a never-ending cycle that has entangled countless hearts.

But Jesus can put you back together again. He can take every broken piece and make you whole. He can successfully operate on your heart and mind and bring transformation through His Word and can restore all that was taken from you. In Him, you can fully trust.

Understand that some are sidetracked because they start out trusting the Lord, but then, if things happen the way that they did not expect or desired, they feel that God and the Word have failed. Many people feel that their failures and mistakes are so bad that they can never be forgiven. Others feel that since they find themselves in situations that others have caused, God must not love them, or they are irrelevant to God.

But thoughts like these do not denote trust. Thoughts like these denote misguided faith. You have more faith in the words of the flesh and in the words of darkness than in the words of God. Your flesh wants to trust what it can see and what it knows. Therefore, it chooses to trust in the tangible things and in temporary pleasures that can momentarily ease the pain.

The enemy wants you to trust every lie and deception that he presents to you. He wants you to look at the situation and think that it is impossible for change to occur. He wants you to think that God does not hear your prayers and that you are not important to God. He wants you to think that your situation is hopeless and that you will never find happiness in your life. He wants you to believe that you will never experience true love and ultimate victory.

Trust in God is different, however. Trust in God does not involve your emotions, because your emotions are unstable and unpredictable. If you feel good, then you believe that God is with you. If you feel bad, then you believe that God has abandoned you. This is not trust in God. Rather, trust in God is knowing, understanding, and accepting His will for your life, believing that no matter what, your life is in His hands. You trust God so much that when things go the opposite of what His promises are to you through the Word, you still trust Him and say, "I realize that the enemy only wants me to stop trusting You." "You are the final authority in my life!"

Understand that when things seem to go in the opposite direction of the promises of God, He is still working it out for your good. It is just deceptive tactics by the enemy to incite you to stop trusting. Despite this, you make the decision to still stand on the Word of God, knowing that His Word does not lie.

Trust is saying that no matter what the struggle is in your flesh, you present your body and mind to God. You know that He will give you the strength through the power of the Holy Spirit to say no to the things that are meant to destroy you. You know that the pain that you feel is temporary and that you were never called by God to stay in hurt and pain, but to live in peace and joy. Therefore, there is an appointed end to your pain. Trust is saying that when things do not go your way, you are still going to trust God, since He knows what is best for you and is still in control of your life.

The problem with trust is that there are those who will not study the Word of God in order to even understand God and in order to understand His promises. The Word of God exposes who God is. How can you trust Him completely if you do not know Him or His will for your life? If you do not have a relationship with God, but rather a one-night stand simply for the benefits of God, then you will not trust Him when things happen contrary to what you expect. How will you know how to decipher what God is allowing for your life at a particular time versus those things that you have the power and authority to spiritually crush and destroy against your life and receive immediate victory over?

Trusting God is not a conditional posture: "If You do this my way, then I will trust You. If You do not, then I will find my own way out." Trusting God is an unconditional posture designed to move on behalf of those who have, first, given their lives to Christ and, secondly, who understand who they are as sons and daughters of God.

Do not look to people, although God does use people in His plan as He wills. People are simply resources or vessels utilized by God. However, you must allow God to be your ultimate source. If you do not allow God to be your source, you may end up confiding in someone who will take advantage of your vulnerability. Jesus is the source, a guaranteed road to wholeness! *You* must want to be made whole and God is the one who can do that.

All the people in the world cannot help someone who refuses to receive the help. You must understand that healing takes place on the inside. Then the results of healing are manifested on the outside in your life. Your focus should be on complete healing of the hurts, rather than seeking a person or vice to help you heal. Sometimes, when you rely on people over God, another person may distract you at the very time Jesus wants to deal with you directly. However, at the time that God desires to send someone to you or lead you to someone in your life as an instrument of direction or counseling, He will. And you will experience the peace of God as confirmation that the person is sent by God.

God is a gentleman. He is not going to move above your will. If you choose to carry burdens, to harbor unforgiveness, or to stroke the pains of the past, God cannot help you. You were created with a free will, and although you may have trouble forgiving or releasing the burden, if you earnestly ask for help, God will be there to help you release the burdens, recover, and be made whole.

It is imperative for you to understand that while you are in a struggle, that is the time when Satan will unleash his predators in search of your vulnerability. He looks for that lonely man or woman. He looks for that rejected youth. He looks for the one with little to no self-esteem left.

Now, you would think that if you are already in a vulnerable state because of situations and battles that left you wounded and battered, the enemy would not continue to stalk you. But, please understand that he is not satisfied with your being only wounded or bleeding. He wants you dead—dead emotionally, dead spiritually, dead in your relationships, and even a premature physical death in a separated state from God and eternal life. Satan's defined mission statement, is to *"...to steal, and to kill, and to destroy"* (John 10:10). He is walking, searching, lurking to and fro seeking whom he can devour. And all it takes is one small opening for him to invade and conquer your life.

Even after you begin to see daylight in your situation, understand that predators lurk. It is the good pleasure of the enemy to ensure that you never enjoy life, never fulfill your purpose in life, never love or are loved and never experience true joy. He will use anyone willing to be used by him in order to ensure that for your life. This is why you must be careful of those that you allow in your life if you are facing hurtful situations (and even when all is well). Not everyone is sent by God to bless you. Some are actually sent by the prince of darkness to destroy you or pull you off track and prevent you from true victory.

Predators seek vulnerability. With predators comes a dimension of control and manipulation. They expect something in return. They expect your allegiance, which ends up meaning your free will. This is a very dangerous situation to be in. With this comes verbal and, many times, physical abuse. With it comes emotional abuse and degradation and even death in various areas of your life. Guard your heart!

Sometimes betrayal comes through those closest to you, those in your inner circle, those who have come to know your weaknesses, likes, and dislikes. Sometimes it comes from those who have studied you. Again, there are predators who will study you to gain your trust and then afterwards strike against you just like a viper. After you have shared your hurts and pain or after you have shared your most intimate secrets with the wrong person, do not be surprised if "Judas" rises up against you. Even in marriage relationships, you can experience hurt or great pain despite all indications that suggested that you would experience love and unity until death.

However, we can see that broken relationships have left people scarred and, sadly for some, scarred for life. But this is a final state that does not have to be. You can choose to be free. Remember, Judas betrayed Jesus, but Jesus called him a friend (Matthew 26:47-50). Judas chose to betray Jesus, but that very act caused Jesus to fulfill His purpose by dying and resurrecting in order for us to be made whole. That is why He addressed Judas as friend. Judas yielded himself to darkness (although he had a choice), yet the purpose of God, through Jesus, was fulfilled through his act of betrayal.

Peter also betrayed Jesus. But the difference is that Peter allowed himself to follow the words of Jesus, and he was delivered and became a great and powerful witness for the Lord. Peter made a choice, and this choice distinguished him from Judas.

Now do not worry about those who allow themselves to be used against you. They are helping you fulfill your purpose. Therefore, you do not have to allow betrayal, hurts, and pain to cause you to bleed profusely for the remainder of your life.

The woman with the issue of blood had been bleeding for twelve long years. The Bible says that she went to every possible person who could help her, but nothing worked. Nobody could help her. The physicians could not help her. Her friends and family could not help her. Then, she became so desperate for healing that she pressed her way through the crowd and touched the hem of Jesus' garment. She believed that if she just touched the hem, she would be made whole. Now that is faith!

Desperate times do call for desperate measures. In her state of bleeding, she was not even supposed to be in the midst of the crowd as she was, because she was considered unclean. However, she was desperate enough to defy. When you are desperate enough, you will do anything you can for deliverance! You will press past the norm. Your actions will supersede the words of others who have told you that "it does not take all of that." And when this woman touched the hem of the garment, the Bible tells us that she was made whole (Matt. 9:20–22)!

People generally do not want to sacrifice the time and effort to crucify the flesh. They will fast only until the next meal but will not do any more than that. They will pray, but they will pray only a surface prayer rather than delve deep into the heart of God. They may give God a five-minute acknowledgment. But in desperate times, you will stay on your knees until you break through and hear from God. Desperation will push you past limits, borders, and boundaries. You may normally study the Word once a month or you may not open your Bible until you go to the next service. However, desperation will cause you to realize that your answer is in the Word because it is unfailing. Your instructions are in the Word. It will cause you to saturate yourself in the Word, knowing your healing and deliverance are in the Word!

Those who are not desperate enough (yet) will say that the Bible is merely words written by men. However, those who are desperate enough will have a sense of understanding to know that the Bible was written by men inspired by God and confirmed through various cross-cultural historical events. They will understand that the prophecies in the Bible have come to pass and that the few that are left are about to take us to eternal rest and blessings or eternal damnation.

The prophecies in the Word are being fulfilled occurring every day in the news and through technology. Yet deception will cause some to still question the Word. Nevertheless, a desperate person will know that the Word of God has power and life. It is simply power and life! Trust God!

Sometimes you may find that the very ones who will acknowledge what God has placed inside of you and will sometimes utilize your gift and anointing, as well as speak greatness over you are also the same ones who will rise against you after you begin to walk in purpose and God's plan for your life. It disturbs them to see your walk take shape and to know that the promises are coming to pass in your life. They can even kill you—kill your dreams and your visions, discourage you from purpose, and destroy your hopes—if *you* allow it. You must hold on to the unfailing words of God for your life! If you want to move out of your ashes, you must ask yourself the question, who can I trust?

First and foremost, you can trust God. Trust Him to give you an inner witness as to whether you should share your dreams, aspirations, hurts, or pain at any given time. Trust God enough to speak to your heart and confirm whether you should be in that relationship. Trust God enough to follow His Word and know that He will lead you to complete wholeness.

People fail in this area because they almost always trust their emotions. Your emotions do not know the future. Your emotions do not know the true heart of another person. Your emotions do not know the struggles you will encounter in life down the road, so it is important to be careful concerning to whom your life is connected.

Too many people are afraid to trust because of their past experiences. But what a blessing it is to be free—free from bondage of the mind and emotions, free to make choices according to God's Word, free to love, free from unforgiveness and free from the guilt of the past!

Trust begins with faith in God, knowing that He is the one who allowed you to be here, and He is the one who has placed purpose in your life. Therefore, whatever challenges arise in your life, you can trust Him to move on your behalf and bring deliverance. You do not have to live in bondage. A free spirit is certainly worth taking the first step of trusting in God. Let your testimony be, "In God, I trust!"

CHAPTER 3

THE *REAL* BATTLEGROUND

Growing up in some churches can predispose you to a false view of relationship with God. Perhaps you heard sermons that made you believe that if you accepted Jesus Christ in your life, your troubles would be few to none. Or perhaps you thought that if you did, blessings would just flow endlessly. Although I did see some believers go through suffering when I was growing up, I cannot recall knowing about too many who went through challenges.

I do remember when some of the older mothers in the church were diagnosed with certain illnesses. Some were healed, and others passed on. Yet they lived in faith and joy, regardless of what happened. They had powerful testimonies of faith or died in the faith, which was encouraging in itself. Yet I just cannot recall hearing too many testimonies of tests and trials, but they, too, went through heartache, hurts, and pain. At that time, issues and challenges were not openly discussed like they are today. Therefore, to me in my young mind, it seemed like everything was always near perfect in their lives.

During those days, there was a distinct separation between children and adults. There was also a distinct separation between saint and sinner, as well as between ministry and laity. Yet with the extent of separation, we were ignorant to most of the struggles or issues that prior generations before us faced. This was just something that was part of that era. But oftentimes I wonder if we would have had to endure some of the struggles that we have gone through as a result of our own wrong choices, ignorance, or the choices of others connected to us if that generation would have shared more of their personal experiences with us.

Today the struggles have intensified. Years ago you may have heard of one or a couple of people going through desperate situations, and everyone rallied in prayer for them. But today almost everyone is confronted with some obstacle, wall, great struggle, hurt, or distress. I am not talking about a typical issue. I am talking about a desperate 911 cry for help!

I am also talking about inner turmoil, emotional distress, and profound burdens. I have never seen such a time when Christians are so desperate that even depression has gripped some of their hearts in astounding numbers. Years ago believers who were facing challenges were considered under the attack of "oppression." We were taught that believers do not get depressed. Today, with so many willing to be transparent in order to help others, we see some believers who actually fight the deadly grip of depression because of all the pressure—and all of this happens while they are sitting in the church and hearing the Word of God week after week! Are we as leaders arming God's heritage to fight and win? You may be able to fault some churches that are not teaching the truth of the Word, but instead let us focus on those churches, pastors, and ministers who are.

Yet there are still those people who choose to remain in bondage, despite avenues of escape. They leave the services, go home, and pamper their pain. Even still, there are those who continue to nurture the pain while sitting in the house of the Lord. How long can you do this without a deficiency occurring somewhere? There will come a time when if you do not choose to let go and move on, you will find that you have backed away from God, completely harboring bitterness and anger. Or you will find yourself in a state of spiritual confusion. You will have backed away from His Word and from church, and you will have even stopped accepting calls from fellow members who just want to show they care.

The enemy loves to divide and conquer. He can speak to you more clearly when you are isolated from your support. In unity, there is strength! As long as you can be kept isolated and segregated, you are weakened, and the battle in your mind and emotions only intensifies.

People are running everywhere to find answers. They are running from conference to conference, from revival to revival, and from service to service. They are running to counselors and tarot card readers; they are reading horoscopes and seeking prophets and false prophets. They are reading self-help books and even Christian inspirational books, and they are attending seminars to improve their self-esteem; but after all of this, innumerable people are still finding themselves embattled in what is probably one of the greatest battles of their lives.

What time is it? What is really going on? Let us take a look at a natural perspective first. The weather and heavens are sometimes unrecognizable. The seasons no longer bear resemblance to what I knew when I was growing up. Back then, the flowers sprang up, the grass turned green, and the trees began to bud in the spring. When I was growing up, the winter was not seventy or seventy-five degrees in my home state. Hurricanes did not come as early and as often and were not as powerful as they are now. It did not rain as much in August in my home state as it has during the last few years. Although we can still discern the seasons because of the time of year, the seasons do show different characteristics from what we were used to years ago. Overall, we are seeing varying types of other storms, such as tsunamis. We see earthquakes in more diverse areas. We see storms with greater disastrous effects and life-changing circumstances.

I find that sometimes although it is still winter, I need to adjust my wardrobe because the weather is much warmer than it should be. Then at other times, I find myself preparing for heavier snowstorms. And when it is still summer and technically I am supposed to be able to plan events until the end of August, I have found that I have sometimes had to adjust my plans within the past couple of years because of the shift in the weather.

Even time has changed. Yes, there are still twenty-four hours in a day, seven days to a week, twelve months to a year, three hundred sixty-five days to a year (excluding leap year), ten years to a decade, and one hundred years to a century; yet time has shortened. Everyone, whether churched or unchurched, believer or nonbeliever, has begun to recognize that time is flying.

The Bible says, *"And except those days should be shortened, there should no flesh be saved: but for the elect's sake those days shall be shortened"* (Matt. 24:22). Jesus said that in order to save those who are His, time must be shortened. Have you noticed that time is moving faster than ever? This was Jesus' response as to signs concerning His impending return. We live in that time.

Because the characteristics of the seasons have changed, I have found that I have also needed to change. Otherwise, I am unprepared or out of sync for what is taking place. Today there are those people who are out of sync with recognizing where the real battle is. In order to use the right response, you must recognize where the real battle is and who the real enemy is. We need to understand that the characteristics of the battles that we are fighting today have changed. Years ago there were struggles, issues, and situations, but it did not seem like the fight was as long or as intense. It did not seem like the pain was as deep. Years ago, in general, people seemingly had to deal with tangible issues; that is to say, issues that could be rectified without the intensity of the struggle of the mind and emotions.

Today because *more* people (not everyone) are blessed with careers, education, and economic resources, the primary issues that plagued many people years ago may not be primary issues today. Answers and resources seem to be more readily available. If you need transportation, you go and get a car. If you need a better job, you go and apply with the backing of your education and experience. Medicine has advanced from years ago (although man's cure for all diseases is still not available).

Although the realities of solutions for issues such as some sicknesses, finance, and family (adoption, divorce, counseling, etc.) may still be tangible ones today for some people, the heightened intensity has shifted and impacted the emotional and mental state of man. For years, if there were marital problems within a family, some considered divorce. But today you have men and women going to the extreme by murdering not only their spouses but also their children. Mental anguish has been fueled with hate, and as we see in the news, the results are deadly. It has magnified itself through multiple issues and circumstances facing any individual at one time. Today the battleground has shifted from the tangible to the intangible field of the mind and emotions.

In the natural, what I see is a shift in what I was used to. What I had accepted as the norm for the season is no longer the norm. And in order for me to continue to be prepared and to excel, I must make certain adjustments.

There is a shift in the spirit realm as well. I believe that what we are experiencing is representative of what is going on in the heavenlies. The spiritual battle that is going on has intensified! The Bible says that the very creation agonizes because of sin (Rom. 8:22). We can see the various transformations in the skies and in the earth. Jesus is soon to come! When He does, it will be wonderful and glorious for those who live according to His Word. But in the meantime, what do we do to survive here?

The only solution is to understand the playing field of the enemy. He moves in deception and that alone. He will either lie or present a partial truth combined with deception, which equals a lie. The Bible says that Satan is the father of lies (John 8:44). Therefore, in order to win against the deceiver, you must understand the playing field, which is the mind.

The Bible says, *"For as he thinketh in his heart, so is he"* (Prov. 23:7). As a human, our perception of what is (reality) generally derives from our senses: *sight, taste, touch, smell,* and *hearing*. The senses are categorized even further. Each area of sense then defines what it represents to our minds. We *see* a commercial featuring a juicy cheeseburger. Then, because of familiarity, our sense of smell signals the mind to recall the *sound* of grilled onions and the *smell* of onions on that juicy cheeseburger. Next, the sense of *taste* causes our salivary glands to be stimulated as our mind recalls the taste of a juicy cheeseburger. Next, we find ourselves either in the kitchen or in the car on our way to the place that makes the best cheeseburgers in town in order to satisfy our senses and *feel* that cheeseburger in our hands, and soon we are satisfied. Isn't it amazing how powerful the mind is?

It is the same principle that dominates the works of Satan. He is successful only through the guise of deception and suggestion, working through your mind and senses. If his thoughts penetrate your mind because you receive them, they are then embedded in your heart. What is in your heart will be demonstrated by your actions and through what you speak. If you receive failure, your actions will demonstrate failure. Everything you touch will fail. You will finally concede to the title of failure. If the voice of the enemy says that you are stuck in your situation and you receive his thought, then you will speak defeat, despair, and hopelessness and will remain in your situation. Defeat, despair, and hopelessness will also manifest in your life.

If you believe in what God says about you and how you were created with a purpose and plan for success, then although you may experience some failure or disappointments, they will end up becoming launching pads for your success. Why? It is because of your perception. If you receive the truth that you are a child of God and that He intends for you to be blessed and live an abundant life according to His Word, then you will begin to exercise trust, develop more faith, believe that He is leading and guiding you, and will have *"good success"* (Josh. 1:8).

Obedience to the Word of God brings good success. However, why do you see so many failures, even in the church? The answer is that there is a condition to being victorious. Victory is not just having countless amounts of money. Victory is not being a celebrity or having a noted title or position. Victory is not having your name in lights or being known all over the world. Victory is achieving abundance in every area of your life by walking in *wholeness,* based on obedience to God and walking in His Word. Victory is a change of mind, resulting in a change of heart, manifested by a change of life!

Success is both knowing and understanding your purpose, walking in it with the love of God in the forefront of your heart. And the Word directly says that in order to have good success, you must obey the statutes of God. Remember, success by God's standards is not success based on man's standards, because many who appear to have success really do not by God's standards. Now I ask you right where you are now, do you have abundant life? If not, do you want it?

Listen to those who constantly say, "I can't" or those who speak negatively about themselves or just have negative attitudes in general. When people are constantly spewing out negativity, this means that negativity is what they are feeding on. It means that Satan is constantly feeding them negativity, and they are constantly digesting it. You are what you eat! Soon the manifestation of bitterness and anger will be seen.

In other cases, the results can be paranoia. For instance, if your perception of everything and everyone is negative, you can also begin receiving false delusions that everyone is out to get you. Nobody likes you. Not only will you look at other things and people in a negative light, but you may also invert these feelings back to yourself and now believe that opposition is always coming against you. Now you have developed a character of negativity and suspicion, and those who do want to excel and grow may soon choose to avoid your negativity and complaining words altogether.

You can become a weight to someone else because of your negative speaking. It is important to hear yourself, examine yourself, and see what is coming out of your mouth. What words are you speaking? Is the first feeling about any situation always a complaint, negative comment, or word of suspicion? If it is, then your mind needs to be renewed in the Word. The renewing of your mind brings about a new attitude, as well as divine wisdom!

The Bible does say that we are not to speak more highly of ourselves than we ought (Rom. 12:3). This is a true word. Otherwise, you will become prideful and arrogant. You will feel that you are the final authority rather than God. But there is a distinct difference between conceit, arrogance, and pride versus knowing who you are in Christ and through Christ.

Jesus knew that He was the Son of God, and He moved and operated in that truth. He also knew His purpose. A powerful device of Satan is for us to misinterpret the humility of Jesus. He was humble in that He submitted to the will of God. But Jesus knew who He was. When He was approached, questioned, and accused by the Pharisees and other spiritual leaders of that day, He provided them with an answer for every accusation that they made against Him (Matt. 16). He did not back down and run into the corner.

Yes, there were times in the Bible where Jesus was led not to speak or answer. But in the times where God released Him, He took a stand and was not intimidated. Why? Because He knew who He was and the authority and power He had. He knew that He had the backing of the heavenly hosts. When Satan tempted Jesus in the wilderness, although Jesus was tired and hungry, He still knew the power of the Word (Matt. 4:1–11). He still knew that He was the Son of God and did not have to yield to the tempting words of Satan.

In order to be victorious, you must know who you are in God. You must know what it means to be a son or daughter of God. Otherwise, when the enemy tries to bombard your mind, you will have nothing to fight with, and your natural intellect and emotions will win against you every time.

The Word of God that renews your mind also brings hope. Without hope, there is no life. As you stand on the Word of God, it may seem like the battle intensifies. It may seem as if it gets more and more difficult to balance your emotions without grasping hold of anger or bitterness. You may even begin to question the direction that God has been taking you, because you may not understand a lot of the challenges that confront you during this time. Nevertheless, always remember that when you surrender hope, you do surrender your life!

Your mind is a very powerful weapon and tool that can be used for your good or against your life. That choice is up to you. The battle against your life can be won if you surrender your mind to those things or people working against the will of God for your life. Since you were created in the image of God, your mind is limitless in its capacity for knowledge, truth, and growth. However, what you do with the knowledge, truth, and growth depends upon you. Do not allow the enemy to capture your mind. When he has your mind, he has you! The next chapter will deal more specifically with the battle of the mind.

CHAPTER 4

WAR OF TWO WORLDS

N ow as the previous chapter stated, the real battleground is the mind. This is why it is imperative to renew your mind, as the Bible says: *"Be ye **transformed** by the **renewing** of your mind"* (Rom. 12:2, emphasis added). To be *transformed* means to "change your makeup or structure." It means "conversion." The transformation begins through regeneration of your spirit through salvation. To *renew* is "to make new"; "to bring back to the original state." Renewing of the mind does not affect only one area of your life, but its penetrable force affects the whole man. Through the Word of God, your mind will be recaptured from the thinking of the world back toward God. In other words, the Word will help you to become more God-conscious than flesh-conscious.

It does not mean that you are so heavenly bound that you are no earthly good. It does not mean that you cannot relate to others here on earth. It does not mean that you are so desensitized through salvation that you have no compassion when others are facing their challenges. It does not license you to forget that you are on earth and are still a fleshly being. However, it does mean that your world, decisions, and choices are aligned with the plan and purpose of God in order to experience abundant life. It does means that you are conscious of the fact that God is the ultimate authority in your life and the final authority over your life. It does mean you are not willing to allow the situation to separate you from God but will allow it to draw you closer to God.

The Word of God will continuously remind you that through the original state of man in accordance with God, all provisions were made. Man had dominion. Man had peace. Man's original state was oneness with God. Man's original state of mind was one of peace and liberty, not bondage and guilt. A renewed mind through the Word can bring you back to oneness (wholeness), dominion, and power.

In Romans 12:1-2 (emphasis added), you are also commanded to *"present your bodies as a living sacrifice, holy and acceptable, which is your reasonable service. And, be not **conformed** to this world."* To *conform* means to "give shape to"; "to contour"; "to be in agreement with." You are commanded to "be not conformed" to the things of this world. This means that you do not allow the world to shape your life. Instead, you allow the Word to shape your life.

The Word of God reveals the character of God. It reveals the mind and power of God. It reveals the strategies of God. Relationship with God will help you understand more about God and His will for your life. It will help you understand your power, authority, and inheritance through Jesus. It will help you win the battle and inner struggles that go on in your life. It will help you understand yourself! Transformation must occur in order for your life to become fashioned in relationship to God's will for your life. Transformation then affects the whole man.

Understand that there is an ongoing battle between your members (physical self) that starts with the mind: *"But I discern in my bodily members in the sensitive appetites and wills of the flesh, a different law (rule of action) at war against the law of my mind (my reason) and making me a prisoner to the law of sin that dwells in my bodily organs, in the sensitive appetites and wills of the flesh"* (Rom. 7:23 AMP). There is a war that is constantly raging between your flesh and your spirit.

Man is three parts: spirit, soul, and body (1 Thess. 5:23). Your spirit relates to the spiritual world and to things of the spiritual realm. Your soul relates to your mind, intellect, reasoning, will, and emotions. Your flesh relates to the natural, or physical, realm.

Your spirit man is the true reality of who you are. When you die (transition from the natural to the spiritual realm), your soul and spirit will live on. If this body was really who you are, then when it died, your existence would cease. However, the spirit and soul do live on. Your spirit houses your soul, with the body as the outer covering. So do not think that when you die and cease to exist from this natural world, it is over for you. It is not!

Isn't it amazing that even for most of those who have other beliefs, most are in agreement that the spirit and soul continue on? If you just ceased to exist, then it really would not matter too much about renewing your mind or ongoing battles, except for motives of material gain and perhaps to live a successful life here on earth. Then, in this world only is where you would receive your reward. This is success that is defined by man.

If you ceased to exist after death, then despite any problems or situations, through death you would never have to face those issues again; and God and His principles would be irrelevant. However, eternity is a long time to guess whether there is truth to afterlife in the presence of God or eternal damnation.

Your spirit will be led either by the Spirit of God or the spirit of darkness, who works in conjunction with the desires of your flesh. Some desires of the flesh are natural but must be kept under subjection with the standards of God. Others are unnatural and are provoked by darkness. Your spirit does not sleep and is not disconnected from the realities of your environment, even when you are not consciously aware. Therefore, the right environment is imperative. Even as you go through life and face those daily challenges, what you feed on will be that which is manifested in your life.

Your body relates to the natural world, which is the physical realm. However, instead of understanding that we are spirit beings housed in natural bodies with souls, most people view themselves according to their physical makeup only. To most, the physical realm seems the most real. Therefore, all decisions are made for the physical benefit; that is, lives are lived for the physical benefit, success and failure are defined by the physical, and the list goes on. However, understanding that you are created in the image of Father

God helps you to realize that you are a spirit being and not eternally flesh.

Again, your soul represents your mind, intellect, reasoning, will, and emotions. Your soul is also a vital part of your being. Many people live by the dictates of their emotions. They rationalize by their intellect and reasoning. However, when yielding to these entities alone, there is no room for faith. These entities can be deceiving in respect to faith. And with respect to the actual battle that takes place between your spirit man and flesh, many people lose to the flesh simply because they hurt and yield to the screaming pangs of their emotions and desperation. But when your soul is fortified with the proper nutrients of the Word of God in conjunction with His ordained purpose for your life, then your soul comes into subjection to your spirit man, who is yielded to the Holy Spirit.

The soul dictates to the flesh. The soul cannot comprehend sacrifice, submission, and discipline on its own. The intellectual properties of the soul will always rationalize the needs of the flesh, regardless of cost. The emotions are always fueled and charged according to a person's rationalization and reasoning. All of this, coupled with the intense desire of the flesh, ignites an explosive war!

If your spirit man is not connected to God and the things of God, then the soul and flesh will win. Sometimes, even when you are connected to God, the battle may seem hard. But if you have continuously fed your spirit man with the things of God—His Word, prayer, living a consecrated life, to name a few things—then the voice of your spirit man will bellow out a familiar song at the time that you need help the most. Your spirit man will come alive just when you are faced with a difficult decision. Your spirit man will provide you with strength to stand on the things that you know are beneficial and not destructive for you. Yes, by the power of the Holy Spirit, your soul can yield to the Word of God.

Now that you understand man's makeup, you should understand that you are a three-part being. The cause of living an imbalanced life is either living it as solely spirit, although you are here on earth, or solely flesh, although the spirit man yearns for the right spiritual connection. This will cause a great imbalance in your life. To live in the flesh only is to never acknowledge being created in the image of a triune (three-part) God: Father, Son, and Holy Spirit. It completely alienates and denies the very part of you that has access to God—your inner spirit man.

Since we are truly spirit beings, our spirit man yearns for communication and fellowship with the spirit realm. This is why in various religions man is constantly seeking for a spiritual connection. To take it further, I believe that since we are created in the image of God, the spirit man is actually yearning for that relationship that it once had with God (in the creation of man).

The spirit of man cries out for relationship with God and desires to live according to the things of God. Have you ever seen such a person, or are you that person who has tried almost everything but still has not found any true satisfaction? That is because true satisfaction comes through divine fellowship with God and living in His perfect will for your life. That is the only thing that can quench the craving that you are trying to feed.

There is temporary satisfaction in the fulfillment of fleshly desires. But when your spirit is satisfied, it will bring complete and lasting peace and joy to your life. It does not mean that you will not experience challenges in life, because you are still in this sinful world. However, it does mean that the Lord will be with you through every challenge in such a way that you can still remain whole, peaceful, and joyous through adversities and struggles.

Understand that your flesh feeds on desires. Have you noticed that the flesh is most satisfied, although temporarily, when it opposes the things of the Spirit? I think Paul said it best: *"I find then a law, that, when I would do good, evil is present with me"* (Rom. 7:21). The flesh's desire is to be contrary to God and all that He represents.

People are looking for fulfillment by going after all that the Word of God opposes. The media profits by portrayals of everything that opposes the principles of God: sexual licentiousness, perversion, dishonesty, and deception. Music videos portray males surrounded by beautiful young, scantily-clad women, who bow to their sexual fantasies, appetites, and whims. They also portray women who are enveloped by young muscular men who are there to yield to their seductions. Marriages, even Christian marriages, are falling apart because of deception, dishonesty, and infidelity. Yet many seek and find (temporary) satisfaction in these things.

The Bible also speaks against deception. There are those who practice lying and deception. Some are actually habitual liars, and it is an embedded part of their lives and their natures. Some have become so accustomed to lying that they lie without cause. Lying is deceptive and dishonest, but this flesh embraces it anytime it feels that it does not want to face truth. Understand that the first victim of deception is the one who is perpetrating the lie. The deception, regardless of how it manifests, first deceives *you!*

Deception feeds through media, entertainment, and daily living. (Thank God for those who are providing alternatives)! Lies filter down through political as well as religious arenas. Again, Satan is the father of lies. The flesh lies for convenience, it lies to boast, and it lies to achieve selfish desires of lust. Because Jesus speaks of truth, lying is a direct defiance of everything that the Lord stands for. Yet it is readily embraced because it is easier for the flesh to choose to lie rather than to face an uncomfortable situation or face the truth.

Covetousness is spoken against in the Word of God. It is the desire to have what someone else has at all costs. This is why people will steal and kill to have what belongs to another person instead of working hard for it themselves. Our society is the embodiment of covetousness. Some people make decisions solely based on the impression it will have on others. Others make purchases simply because they cannot stand the thought of someone else obtaining any attention, through material gain.

Jealousy and envy generally accompany covetousness. In some neighborhoods, one homeowner may do something to improve his property. Then another homeowner may suddenly feel the need to surpass it. To be inspired because someone else does something positive is great. However, to do something with the intent of down-playing another's actions or blessings and to despise the fact that someone else has done something positive or received a blessing are in opposition to the heart and character of God. There is an obvious inner issue of insecurity in the one that practices this behavior. The battle is strong in your mind when you have chosen to live like this and cannot be happy for another.

The Word of God commands us, *"Thou shalt have no other gods before Me"* (Ex. 20:3). This is to say that we are to respect God as number one in our lives. Yet anything and everything else have taken the place of God in hearts and lives today—material possessions, money, careers, family, friends, opportunity, and prestige, just to name a few.

Even religion itself has taken the place of relationship with almighty God! People have chosen to let religious tradition become their god over intimacy with the true and living God. This is evident when the priorities of the services are anything and everything but God and souls. It is also evident with leaders who are not following the glory cloud. Some leaders would rather follow personal agendas than follow the voice of God, which would benefit His people. It is evident with the priority of prestige and glamour over souls.

The war between the spirit and the flesh is an intense battle that entangles your desire to be satisfied, comforted, and fulfilled with immediate gratification versus the moral and spiritual compass to do what is deemed to be right according to the Word of God. The flesh always looks for immediate gratification. It craves and longs for satisfaction and is impatient in receiving it. The flesh is like a temperamental child who sees what it wants and goes after it, never considering the consequences.

The fleshly desires intensify when the mind incites the physical yearning by constantly recalling and rehearsing the pleasures and satisfaction of accomplishing its targeted goal in order to experience the expected end. Although some desires are natural, if left unbalanced they can cause you to follow the deceiving thoughts and emotions of the flesh in order to obtain them. For Instance, it is a natural desire to want to prosper and succeed economically. However, it is a deceiving thought that would lead one to gain any economic advantage by breaking the law. It is a natural desire for a woman to want a child. Yet it is thoughts of deception that would cause a woman to go to the hospital and take another woman's baby just to satisfy her yearning. It is a natural desire to want a spouse. However, it is deceptive thinking that would cause one to manipulate and break up another's home in order to get one. All actions and seeds sown against the principles of God will reciprocate that same type of return in the life of the offender.

The flesh is unreliable in that it almost always wants to follow its emotions. Its emotions follow its thoughts. Its thoughts follow its reasoning and senses. The flesh is incapable of understanding spiritual principles, except through the voice of the Holy Spirit. And because of this, the Bible says that the flesh is enmity (the enemy) of God. It is enmity because it is selfish and unwilling to submit to the spiritual laws that have been put in place to ensure life in abundance. Its refusal is because it knows that this means personal sacrifice.

Many of you may be able to recall a time when you thought that you were strengthened enough to conquer this flesh. Then you found yourself in a situation where you realized that you alone could not conquer this flesh. Granted, some people are naturally disciplined in some areas. However, only through submission to the Holy Spirit are you able to conquer this flesh.

The flesh's power is through your mind and senses. The mind can launch you three thousand miles away while you are still seated in your room. The images created in your mind can seem so real that your body, the physical you, begins to react to certain thoughts. The mind is so powerful that you can recall incidents or information that you stand assured on as truth, only later to find out when truth is revealed that you were wrong. The mind can make wrong appear as right. Never underestimate the power of the mind working in conjunction with this flesh!

The Word of God commissions you to walk after the Spirit and not after the flesh. When you accept the Lord as your Savior, your spirit has then come into agreement with and surrendered to the Spirit of God. Your spirit is then regenerated. However, in order to continually walk in newness, your mind must be renewed through the Word of God. Some people receive instantaneous deliverance from their struggles. However, for others, since the soul is the seat of emotions that deal with the mind and intellect, these areas still need renewing.

The mind recalls and rehearses what is familiar until other thoughts replace the past. In order to keep from going back to those things of familiarity from your past that were detrimental to you, you need to fuel your inner man with the Word of God and with positive seeds. This gives you ammunition when temptation comes. The Bible gives you the map to abundant life and wholeness. Therefore, your soul needs to be fueled with those things that will bring you life. A person can profess having a renewed mind until Jesus comes, but real evidence of having a renewed mind is in direct correlation to that person's character and life.

Having a renewed mind will prevent you from having a stale and stagnant life. Renewing of the mind will yield fruit. It is not yielding and receiving the bondage of the mind. It is not dwelling in defeat. The Word is life! So you cannot digest the Word without the manifestation of "life" in your life. That is because God is life! His words are life!

The evidence is in the fruit that you bear. Quoting Scriptures is not enough. There are those who will quote Scriptures and think that things are supposed to magically fall into place. Then they get discouraged when their lives never change and cycles are never broken. But in order to see results, you must *apply* the Word and not just quote it! To apply is to put received revelation (exposed/revealed knowledge) into action. Application is action after true revelation is revealed and grasped. You cannot have a renewed mind without the manifestation of life! A change in your soul—your mind, intellect, reasoning, will, and emotions—will result in victorious living and new life.

Through your spirit man, you can commune with God in prayer. Also, through your spirit man, you will receive answers from God. He will cause an impression upon your heart as a confirmation to you. And confirmation can also come through Scripture, another person, or something that you heard or read. Regardless of the method or vehicle, if you recognize the voice of God, you will feel that peace and comfort that accompanies His voice.

In various instances in my life, I have received a check in my spirit letting me know that the enemy had risen in some way against me, my family, or friends. I would then evaluate my posture of prayer in faith against the enemy and his devices and would be victorious. Hearing God has been a blessing to my life and to the lives of others.

As discussed, our human nature relates to two worlds, the natural and spiritual. It is when those two worlds collide that we have chaos and confusion. There is a part of us, the spirit man, that cries out to do right. But there is also the natural man that wants what it desires. It does not care about the future and consequences of actions it may take. It cares only about here and now, which is why it constantly seeks selfish and fleshly gratification. Thus we have the war of two worlds.

The mind is so powerful that it filters throughout your being everything that you feed it. Whatever you digest, good or bad, will be filtered throughout your spirit, soul, and body. Your mind seems like it is like one of those computers in the movies that suddenly begins to act, think, and make choices on its own without the aid of its creator, man. Your heart may have one way of thinking and your mind another. You may desire to do what is right, according to your deepest instincts. But your mind may reason you to yield to another desire (of the flesh).

Remember, if your mind is fed those things against the nature of God, it will begin to feel that it does not need any part of God. Deception is a powerful tool of the enemy that works along with your flesh and soul. Satan will speak to your emotions and senses in hope of seeing the manifestation through your flesh. In other words, what he provokes you to think and accept will result in strengthening the desires of your flesh. Then once your feelings and senses are ignited, your flesh (body) will align. This will result in the manifestation of that thought that you received. Remember, as he did with Adam and Eve, Satan will never let you know the consequences of wrong choices. He will simply present seductions to you, understanding the physical needs of man and his desire to have immediate gratification and satisfaction.

In James 1:8, the Bible says that *"a double-minded man is unstable in all of his ways."* This chapter is admonishing you to go through your challenges in life by faith. It is admonishing you to not waver, but to be steadfast in your hope. Also, in the natural aspect, instability in your mind will affect your decision making, which results in a negative or destructive lifestyle, including loss. When a person is consistently wavering in decision making, you will see the manifestation in his life.

A double-minded man (or woman) cannot rationalize his choices. He will consistently make the wrong decisions. His decisions will be based on feelings, emotions, and familiarity. It will be based on fear or other factors that govern his decisions, rather than on informational guidance or spiritual guidance. A double-minded man will be inconsistent in his actions, words, and promises. His life will reflect the weight that he carries rather than reflect one who has built his own life and helps build the lives of others.

When there is a consistent negative cycle in your life, you must recognize the root cause. Is this the result of your environment? Are you living under a generational curse? Is your pain due to a soul tie that has not been broken? Understanding God helps you understand yourself. And in understanding yourself, you will then begin to identify the root causes of the problems in your life.

The root is that which is conceived in the mind—bondage or freedom. And when you decide that you want to be free, you will then see the war that rages: a desire to be free versus the bondage of the flesh. Yet God is with you.

After the root is identified, then you can uproot and move on with new thinking. Uprooting is a process of understanding who you are destined to be. It is understanding God's will for your life. It is the renewal of the mind through the Word of God. It is consistent prayer and learning of biblical principles, along with the application of those principles. It is even utilizing productive resources and counseling to help turn your life around. It even consists of separation from those who would still hold you in bondage.

What you are doing is saturating your life with the richness of growth, expansion, maturity, morality, wisdom, and spiritual fortitude. This process will drown out all the sinful contaminants, your past, constricting vices, guilt, and any other form of captivity that once restrained and suffocated your life. This process brings resiliency in order to resist those things that once held you captive. This is transformation.

The beginning of transformation is the acceptance of new seeds. Nonbelievers might not use the Word of God to renew their minds;

however, there is an abundance of success stories where they have renewed their minds through self-help resources, career development, weight control, specialized training, or psychological counseling and have been able to see massive changes in their lives. People have grabbed hold of the simple principle of mind renewal, and countless lives have changed in some ways.

But you must understand the benefits of renewing your mind with the Word as well. The advantage that you have when using the Word of God as a foundation is that the Word penetrates the spirit, soul, and body, and God's divine guidance will positively affect and benefit your whole man in His divine purpose and plan for your life. Additionally, in these cases, the success will bring glory to God as you reap the bountiful benefits. Renewal through the Word brings eternal results, not just natural results. When your mind is renewed in the Word, you can lose everything and still be restored, knowing that God's will for your life is abundance and wholeness in every area of life.

Another aspect of battle is when you struggle in accepting that the promises and inheritance of God are for you. There are those who will accept the Lord Jesus Christ as their personal Savior yet live beneath their privilege because they feel that the blessings are for others and not themselves. The natural man can convince you that you are not worthy of God's blessings because of your past. You cannot listen to the voice of doubt, but rather you must listen to the voice of God through His Word.

There are also those who will accept only some of the blessings because they allow logic to reason them out of other blessings. In other words, they will stand on their limitations or limited resources rather than stand on the promises of God. If others are being blessed with homes, then why can't you receive yours? Perhaps a young lady will be willing to receive the blessing of a good job, yet she cannot believe that God will bless her with a good husband. Some of you will stand and applaud the pastors and ministers as they preach hope in the Word, yet you will not apply that same Word. You will attend conference after conference and read book after book but yet not stand on the Word of God for yourself!

I recall a conversation in which a minister was speaking about the fact that God has ordained a way out of poverty. Afterward someone responded by saying, "But the Bible says that the poor will always be among us" (Mark 14:7). This person had grabbed hold of this Scripture and decided that it must be God's will for him to be poor. Instead, he could have chosen to accept Jesus' mission statement for his life: *"...I have come that they might have life and that they might have it more abundantly"* (John 10:10). Then, as he walks in God's revelation and blessings for his life, he could have gone back to the others who remain in a poverty state and showed them a way out.

Your mind, again, is so powerful that it can dictate your state of life; and if it sides with reason or misinterpretation of the Word, this can cause you to miss out on what God desires for your life. This man's tongue sealed his open door to a way out of his financial bondage. Everyone may not be a millionaire; however, you also do not have to live from paycheck to paycheck. You can choose to expand your mind through its renewal in the Word of God, or you can stay in bondage.

Some people struggle with acceptance and find that there is a battle that rages within them to even feel that they are worthy of anything that God has for them. Your perception of yourself must be aligned to what God says about you. In other words, you might not see all that God has proclaimed you to be, but by faith you must receive and walk in who He says you are! In aligning yourself with who God has proclaimed you to be, then you will find it easier to receive the things that God has for you. Understanding that He is a loving and forgiving God and that your past is no longer an issue will eradicate any doubt that He wants the best for you.

You must understand that you are created in the image of God and, therefore, have become his son or daughter. This means that you have a kingdom of inherited wealth in the Lord! You can experience the richness of your inheritance in your family, your health, your mind, your emotions, your finances, and in all areas of your life.

It does not mean that life will not challenge you. But it does mean that you will not fight the battle of faith alone when you belong to God. It does mean that you have the support of God. Do not allow the battle in your mind to cause you to live in defeat. Remember, your mind is fertile ground, and the seeds that you sow there are the seeds that will spring up into a great harvest. So read the Word of God for yourself so that you will understand that God is delighted to bestow blessings upon your life when you live according to His Word (Deut. 28).

When you renew your mind through the Word of God on a consistent daily basis, the mind then receives more and more of an understanding of who you are in relationship to God. The Word lets you know how important you are to God and that you are not just here by chance. It lets you know that you were created with purpose. The Word of God lets you know that God has great blessings for you in accordance to your walking in His perfect will.

The Word empowers you! When you read about the power of God and revelation of truth, when you read about the great victories won by God for His people, when you read about how Jesus defeated Satan through His death and resurrection and that he will be destroyed eternally after Jesus returns, you will then have a greater appreciation for and trust in God. When you hear the testimonies of those around you and when you reinforce God's goodness and greatness, His power and glory, His limitless love for you, then you begin to understand that there is nothing more valuable than your relationship with God. When you experience the peace and joy of God, when you read about all the promises that He has provided for you in His Word, you begin to understand that true safety and abundant life come through Jesus Christ.

When you even remember what God has already done for you, as you read His promises, you come to love Him in such greater depth. This love that you develop goes beyond material blessings; it is such a depth of appreciation just for Him being as great as He is in your life! You begin to appreciate Him for being God and for being your Father. You begin to appreciate Him for providing hope rather than allowing you to stay entrapped. You begin to love Jesus even more for enduring all that He did on the cross for you.

You then realize that all the opposition and distractions that rose up against you and all the ashes that you were left to face are ineffective compared to the healing power of God. You begin to realize that the Word of God is truly life and that the battle between the two worlds will always lead you to a confrontation of choice. If you make the right choice, then you will experience the true victory that was intended for you!

CHAPTER 5

LOST IN TRANSITION

Transition is defined as "passage"; "change"; "development". A *passage* is "a way of exit or entrance." It is a way out of the old and into the new, out of the past and present and into the future, out of your pain and into your promise. Finally, it is a way out of your training season into purpose and your destined place.

It is amazing how we say, "Lord, increase in me"; "Lord, have Your way"; "Lord, use me for Your will and glory." Yet we resent the passage to expansion. Many times we even speak against what God is doing because it does not feel good or because it is inconvenient and uncomfortable. When we do not understand what God is doing, we immediately begin to allow frustration and anger to fill our hearts and replace our trust.

Basically, we will trust Him as long as it feels good to us. We will trust Him as long as we see the blessings. We will trust Him as long as we can hear Him speak. We will trust Him as long as we understand what He is doing and where He is taking us. But how much do we trust Him when we don't see?

Examining this further, when you trust God based on feelings, in reality you have basically told God that He can have His way in your life as long as there is no inconvenience to you. You have told the Lord that you will yield to Him and allow Him to increase in your life, in your walk, in the anointing, as long as it does not make you feel uncomfortable and as long as you do not have to sacrifice. However, you must remember that any passage to birth is not comfortable or convenient.

Inception

The passage to any birth is painful. But there is a process that, if you understand, will help you endure the pain through to birth. The first part of the life process is inception. God has implanted a seed of purpose in your life. You were called to purpose before you were born.

However, the seeds that you carry need to be cultivated. They need to grow. They need to develop. They need to be nurtured. During the various situations you encounter throughout your life, the Lord will use those situations as an occasion to cultivate the seed that He has implanted in your life. To *cultivate* means "to prepare"; "to foster growth through labor to refine or improve."

What is the direction for your life? What is your passion? What are your gifts and talents? Have you noticed that at various stages in your life, you have always been pushed in a certain direction? Or have you noticed that when you try to move away from certain areas, careers, or talents, you are always directed back? For example, teachers may have found themselves constantly desiring to be around children to teach and impart, even before they reached a point of deciding to become a teacher. Singers may have had the experience of singing before their families and friends while growing up. Then they may have had opportunities to participate in school or church choirs. Finally, as that seed continued to grow from the nurturing, the singers found themselves walking in their call. To nurture is to feed. The feeding brought forth growth.

In other instances, God will use your pain to water your seed. In some cases, there are women who were raised by someone other than their mothers. For some reason, they ended up in foster care or at a relative's house to be raised. Because of their experiences, they grew up and opened their hearts and many times their homes to others. Some chose professions based on their desire to help estranged youth. Their hearts carried the pain of others because of their experiences, and they turned it around to give life and hope to others. Anytime God uses the opportunity to feed that seed within, it will grow, develop, and take you into purpose.

As you carry the seed, you will go through various changes, naturally, spiritually, psychologically, and emotionally. You will experience the emotional pinnacles and plunges, the ups and downs. That is because Satan wants you to abort the seed; that is to say, to destroy through rejection what God desires for your life. He wants you to choose his way over God's way.

There are those people who have died with purpose...gifts, talents, skills, abilities that they never tapped into because they aborted the seed. There are those people who rejected God and ended up in an early grave or in degradation. Perhaps if many would not have made the choice to disobey God, they would not have experienced unnecessary pain or hurts in their lives. Perhaps the relationship that caused a broken heart would never have taken place if they had taken heed to God for their lives.

Severing your relationship with God rejects the plan for your life. Yes, God's mercy is extended, and so is His grace. But there comes a time when wrong choices can destroy your life and the seed that you carry. To treasure and appreciate the seed God has planted means that you will do all that you can to see that it grows, develops, and comes forth.

Carrying

Carrying the seed gets tiring sometimes. You can get weary sometimes. While you are carrying, your seed grows, and there is more to you than there was before. When you get to the place that God begins to acknowledge who you are, do not think that everyone will be happy for you. When He is preparing to take you to another place, do not think that everyone will celebrate you. There are those who will try to cause you to miscarry. This is a tactic of the enemy.

Since you did not choose to abort, Satan will use anything or anyone willing and available to cause you to lose your seed. They will rise up in criticism: "Why is he doing this?" "Why does she have to do it that way?" Others will feel threatened because of the fact that you have chosen to obedience to God for *your life!* See, there are those who will embrace you as long as you conform to their expectations and insights for your life. But as soon as you begin to stand on your own two feet and trust God for yourself, as well as develop a personal and intimate relationship with God, others who have not chosen that way will become threatened.

There are even those Christians who may mean well, but they have put God into a box—if you will allow me to use that expression—and they have tied God's hands. What I am trying to say is that they will trust God only in what they know. They will not move into unfamiliar ground. They will limit God for their lives. They will not trust their relationship with God to allow Him to cause them to excel, and they will resent you for doing so. Some will call you prideful or rebellious—anything to cause you to back away, turn around, stop you from walking in fruition of what God has planned for your life. It is a sad thing, but some people have allowed fear to overrule faith. Then they allow Satan to use them to launch attacks against you so that you will not fulfill the purpose that God has for your life.

Have you ever studied the behavior of those who habitually lash out against others? Looking at the psychological and sociological perspectives can provide you with a clarion view of their lives. Having an infertile mind (no vision), negative environmental influences, or distorted views can sink people to such an abyss that as they see you move forward in life, their only satisfaction is lashing out at you.

What you learn by behavioral observation can help you gain certain insights into human behavior from a natural perspective. Then, in seeing through the eyes of the Spirit, you will gain more of a complete profile as to why abusers choose the actions and paths that they do. I believe that for every action, there is a spiritual inciting behind it. First, those who have received their orders from the enemy and launch attacks against you are really launching attacks against God. So they are already defeated.

Next, these individuals spend excessive amounts of time plotting against your life because of their own issues. They do not realize that they are digging themselves deeper into the pit that they meant for you. Have you ever seen anyone dig a ditch? Well, in digging, you do not find yourself still standing at the top of the pile of dirt as the ditch grows deeper. You find yourself right there in the midst of the ditch. So understand that the weapons and attacks launched against you will soon be returned to the sender and will manifest against their own life.

The spiritual principles are still in operation. You will reap what you sow (Gal. 6:7). These people will always stay stagnant or even lose their place and miss their purpose when they allow themselves to be used by the enemy. Sometimes it can appear that they prosper, but the Word say, *"Fret not thyself because of evildoers, neither be thou envious against the workers of iniquity. For they shall soon be cut down like the grass, and wither as the green herb"* (Ps. 37:1–2).

When people launch against you and wish you failure, they have determined the type of consequences that will manifest in their own lives. Further, when those who profess Christ allows themselves to be used by the enemy, they are either living with a false profession in that they have not really surrendered their hearts to God, or they have opened a door to darkness somewhere along the line and stand in need of deliverance before it is too late. They walk in disobedience, because the Holy Spirit will let them know what they are doing or saying that is against the very heart of God.

When individuals operate like this, there are certain demonic spirits that are in operation: intimidation, low or no self-worth, jealousy, insecurity, or pride. It can be a combination or all of these. Such people have allowed these spirits to rule their lives. Yet you are obligated to pray for them, as Jesus prayed for those who crucified Him. Why? Praying for them helps ensure that you maintain a forgiving heart so that you can continue to grow and reap the benefits of God. So understand that when opposition comes through those "brothers" or "sisters" who profess Christ, there are other issues working in their lives, and what you are experiencing is simply a manifestation of what is inside of them. You just be sure that *your* heart stays pure! Whether you are a believer or nonbeliever, when you allow yourself to be used to bring hurts and pain to another, the consequences will be the same for you—defeat.

When individuals profess Christ but allow themselves to be used by the enemy, they are living in denial of their own true internal struggles. Their negative actions toward you are directly indicative of their own inner struggles. They justify themselves with deceptive thinking. In other words, because they say they love you, in their mind that justifies the negative and sometimes abusive actions that they take against you. Remember, God always looks at the heart! Justification of their ungodly behavior rests within their own minds, under the influence of deception.

Many times some of the ones smiling in your face are in secret speaking words of death over your life. *"Out of the abundance of the heart, the mouth speaks"* (Matt. 12:34). They must realize that when they speak words of death against you, they have spoken against the divine purpose of God for your life and have therefore spoken against God. So now the real battle is between them and God, and God always wins! This means that you are secure in Him, and as long as you are willing to follow His divine purpose, you will not fail, no matter what has been said or done against you. Understand, it is all a plot of the enemy to cause the pressure against you to be so great that it causes you to miscarry.

Again, the Word of God lets us know that the very seed that we have sown will come back to us, *"Be not deceived; God is not mocked: for whatsoever a man soweth, that shall he also reap"* (Gal. 6:7). In the book of Obadiah, when the descendants of Esau (Edom) sat and watched their brothers, the descendants of Jacob (Judah), suffer and spoke against them, God turned calamity and suffering back upon Edom's head. Then He prospered Jacob's descendants. So anyone who comes against God's anointed is in battle with God!

Therefore, it is important for you to examine yourself to make sure that your heart is pure. Otherwise, you will never see the divine purpose as God intended and will simply settle for crumbs in your own life. This is a spiritual principle of God that does not change for anyone. And always remember, *"The battle is not yours, but it is the Lord's"* (2 Chron. 20:15).

Understand that while you are carrying and although you may experience the weight of the seed, God will help you through to birth, as long as you allow Him to. Do not allow anyone to cause you to lose your seed. So do not miscarry, but go through!

Labor Pains

Right at the time before birth, you will experience your greatest pain. The battles will intensify. There are times that you may experience rejection, loneliness, or betrayal. There are times when you will feel that things cannot get worse. Then, before you know it, it does! There may be times when you ask yourself, "Where is God?" Now you are at the point to where you are preparing to bring forth. It may not look like it or feel like it. But now is not the time to give up. You have gone through the inception, the nurturing, and the development. You have carried to full term, but you still need to *push with the pain!*

Now you have got to actually labor for your victory. Labor for your increase! Labor for the birth and promise! Remember, transition is a passage, or way of exit or entrance. You are now preparing to exit from the old and birth forth in the new. You are now experiencing the greatest birthing pangs, your greatest suffering, your greatest pressure. Here you may feel like you absolutely cannot go on. Here your mind and emotions may repeatedly cry, "I cannot take any more." Here the cycle of hurts, obstacles, or distress has gripped you endlessly. Here the enemy will keep telling you, "Why bother?" He will rehearse everything that has happened—every disappointment—in order to create a picture that standing in faith does not work. Yet you still have to push! You have got to labor and fight through to victory!

The place of transition is where many people lose out. This is the place where many choose to turn their backs on God and let go of truth. This is the place where many choose to obey the dictates of the flesh and make their own way out. Here they turn their focus away from the weapon and the fact that it shall not prosper to focus instead on the weapon forming.

You are tired of hurting. You are tired of waiting. You may have even come to the place where you feel like you do not want anyone to remind you of your prophecies, or you do not want to hear another prophecy. You just want to see the manifestation of the promise. You just want relief for your flesh!

But ask yourself a question. If you do not trust God, in whom do you trust? If you come to a place to where you want to give up and you do, then in whom will you trust? Can you trust your intellect over the voice of God? Can you trust your reasoning over the instructions of God? Can you trust your own abilities over the hand of God? Is your way working? Do you have peace? Do you have joy? Is your intellect your strength? Is your reasoning working over the Word and favor of God?

Those you see soaring today and operating in wholeness are those who have made it through transition. They stuck it out! They waited on God! And every one of them has a story. Countless people have reasoned themselves out of their blessings. They have been deceived simply because of being directed by emotions. They have lost their blessing and missed their purpose because they found trust in self and reasoning over God. A spiritual battle needs spiritual strategies. So the answers must come through your spirit being connected to the Spirit of God— not through your flesh!

Your flesh will always tell you to do something contrary to God if it will make you comfortable. Your flesh will always look for a way out so you will not be inconvenienced. Why do you think so many false religions exist with so many followers? Because they do not ask you to sacrifice greatly! You can do anything you want but not have to worry about accountability. With some, the primary focus is self-gratification and self-aggrandizement. You are taught to set your own destiny. Understand that true success is obedience to God, because when you walk in victory, then God gets the glory as you experience the blessing. This is based on the purpose He has destined for you.

Purpose is assigned for the benefit of mankind. Even nonbelievers can walk in some form of purpose when they accept their gift or call. There are those who were created to invent. Others were created to lead. There are great people to whom we can attribute countless innovations. There are those who have introduced various medical breakthroughs, all for the benefit of mankind and to make a difference. Not everyone is called to the four walls of the church. And many of these people have all been noted for their accomplishments. But not all of them attributed their success to God.

The difference is that when you walk in the divine purpose of God, your success will bring glory to God as your life lines up with the Word of God while you also bless others. You understand that divine purpose is not just for your benefit, but it will inevitably point others to almighty God and the life He offers. This divine plan benefits the whole man. The divine plan of walking in purpose does not just benefit the natural man, but it also benefits the spirit man. The divine plan brings wholeness to your life and to others. Therefore, during your painful experiences, you must stay focused on the divine plan for your life.

Since there are those who attribute success to an abundance of finances, let us look at this perspective. Remember that many high-profile people generally do have wealth. Top business leaders, athletes, political figures, and celebrities, to name a few, are wealthy, but many have sexual addictions, drug addictions, eating disorders, unstable relationships, broken homes, or end up committing suicide. Why? Generally, it is because in some part of their lives, they are trying to camouflage issues and pain. They use the vehicles of resource and accessibility to try to forget their pain. These vices, however, are both temporary and self-destructive.

But help is in the Word of God. Again, understand Christ's mission statement: *"I have come that you may have life and that you may have it more abundantly"* (John 10:10). God sent His only begotten Son so that we can have abundant life! But abundance is not measured by your bank account alone. Many wealthy people are spiritually and morally bankrupt. They do not have peace. They do not have joy. They do not have love. They mistakenly feel like they can buy these things. There is nothing wrong with wealth, but understand that with wealth, if you are not whole, you only become more of what you already are.

Instead, abundance is found in being whole. Will you be made whole? This will come only through Jesus Christ. He came, suffered, died, battled Satan and won, and rose again so that you would not have to die. You may look at your life and see nothing left but a pile of ashes. But Jesus has the power to resurrect you right out of your ashes!

Never accept the lie that your lot is to remain in suffering. Do not embrace the lie that in your situation, there is no way out. No! You must fight! You must contend for the prize! You do not have to walk around with a façade of life when in actuality you have given up and are "living" a life of death.

A corpse can appear to have life in the rigor mortis stage. It may move a limb or even sit up because of contracting muscles. However, in actuality, there is no life. It is a corpse because the spirit and soul of that man are gone. During the transitional period, you must be careful that you do not become as the walking dead. You can look like you are functioning in your daily capacity, but in reality you are dead because you have given up hope.

One day the Lord gave me a dream in which I was driving in a neighborhood past a local church. After I passed the church, the Lord said, "Pull over; park and just watch. I want to show you something." As I turned the car around and watched the church, I began to see what looked like people coming from the parking lot and walking to the church. They were talking with one another, had big Bibles in their hands and dress clothes on, and were walking toward the front of the church.

But as I continued to watch, I began to notice that these were not actually living beings. They were disembodied spirits—dead beings dressed as living beings holding Bibles and briefcases. They were dead beings preparing to come together to get their weekly religious fix. They were the walking dead. They represented churchgoers— religious churchgoers—who were not alive, but dead. They were showing up for service week after week. They were dressed in their finest apparel for the occasion. They had their Bibles in their hands but did not experience the life that comes through the Word. They were dead.

This was a representation of too many churchgoers and their spiritual state. They go through the motions of spirituality; however, there is no substance or depth to their lives. They merely live a façade rather than develop a true relationship with God. They accept death, when they could walk in life, wholeness, restoration, and newness.

It is vital that you are not disconnected from your life support during the transition. That is to say again, stay in the presence of God. When pain abides, instead of running closer to God, there are those who have a tendency to run away from God. They have the inclination to blame God. They soon speak against the things of God until doubt replaces trust.

When the spirit of a man is gone; that is to say, his dreams, hope, faith, trust, there is nothing left but death. This is why it is imperative to stay connected to the source — God! I remember one day when I was in a hurry and printed something on the computer. But in my haste, I was not thinking, and I shut the computer down in the middle of the printing. The printing stopped. Being disconnected from the power source caused the printing to stop. I thought that I could power up the computer again and that it would automatically start printing from where it had left off. Well, I did power it up, but it did not start printing again. I selected "print" again, and it still would not print. Then I went into the print queue and deleted the previous prompts for print. Only then was the line clear again.

I knew that stopping and restarting the printer had worked at other times, but this time not until the line was cleared did the print resume. I thought that I could start printing from where I had left off when I powered up again, but I could not print until there was a direct power source and the obstructions were deleted. Only when you stay connected to the source and remove those barriers and hindrances will you begin to operate in the true liberty that God has ordained for your life.

While in transition, you may experience a pruning from God. He will take the opportunity to prune you and get rid of those things that will hinder your growth and development. Pruning does not feel good, because there is a cutting away. If there are things from your past that need to die, then transition is the time when God will use the opportunity to further develop you.

When you care for a plant and see that some leaves are brown, you cut them off. You do not want death to filter throughout the entire plant. Instead, you want to ensure that there is a flow of growth without any hindrances. Understand that what you did on yesterday cannot always work for today and tomorrow. How you did something yesterday may not work today or tomorrow. What you nursed and embraced in the old cannot go into the new. This is the pruning or cutting of those things that would wrap themselves around you like a python in order to strangle and destroy you or hinder you from ever reaching your fullest potential. It may hurt, but allow God to prune you. It is for your own good.

When you are caring for a plant, if you do not water it, it will die. Water your life with the Word of God. Pray the Word of God! Stand on the Word of God! Let the rain of the Holy Spirit drench your life as God takes you through your transition period. Chase after God! Stay in the presence of God!

God cannot afford to have your old attitudes in this next dimension of His plan for your life. He cannot afford to allow you to carry those old wounds into this next phase of your life. God cannot afford to allow you to hold on to that limited mind-set. He has to bring forth more of what He has placed inside of you. He must bring you to a place where you have moved into that destined place of divine purpose.

God is a supreme and masterful physician. He operates with precision and accuracy. He is not like man. He will not cut away vital parts of you. He is not trying to destroy you, but to develop you. If you are not developed, you will not be able to hold on to the blessings that God is about to bestow upon you. You will not be able to handle the next phase and all that comes with it in the next place. Development and maturity keep out pride, arrogance, control, and other forms of dark and negative manifestations that have caused man to turn his back on purpose. Development will enable you to war against the enemy and win as he stands up against you, even after you receive your blessing.

Understand that your blessing is connected to purpose. It is time to look past just the material blessings. Yes, those are wonderful, and thank God for those types of blessings, because they are needed and appreciated. But first things first: *"Seek ye first the kingdom of God and His righteousness and all these things shall be added"* (Matt. 6:33). There are blessings of character building too. When God operates on you, His desire is to remove those things that will stifle your complete development.

God wants to bring you to a place where you totally trust Him. Always acknowledge Him to direct your path (Prov. 3:6). God will use situations of life that have come your way to teach you to trust Him, to bring spiritual development, and to increase your faith. If you are submitted to God, all of this and more will happen and will benefit *your* life.

If you do not submit to God but choose to do it your way, you are missing out on one of the greatest blessings of your life. God desires to use your situations to bring you to a place where you are immune to those things that distracted and lured you in the past. When you have victory over that thing that held you in the past, then you have evidence of your growth and development. There are those people who need deliverance from issues and do not even realize it. They have accepted the poisons that filter through the veins of their lives and have not even understood that they have. They have accepted that they are prisoners, enslaved to mediocrity or degradation. Others no longer care that they have accepted defeat, because to them it is easier to give up rather than fight. There are those people who have made the choice and have accepted Jesus Christ into their lives but have not allowed themselves to be healed and delivered from bondage and baggage. Their spirit man is new in the Lord, but their soul is still embracing those things it is familiar with.

Deliverance can be a process for many people. There are those who have accepted Jesus and their taste for anything detrimental from their past died immediately. But then there are others who have accepted Jesus but still have the old mind-set and therefore remain susceptible to reaching back to that which they are familiar with. This is also because of the depth of the sin to which they gave themselves, as well as generational curses and soul ties.

The renewing of the mind comes through the Word of God and embracing kingdom principles designed for your success. It comes from learning more about God and understanding who He created you to be. It comes from joining in fellowship with other believers who speak life to you. It comes from constantly communicating with God in prayer, praise, and worship. Again, it will come by understanding that Satan's mission statement is to steal, kill, and destroy. His mission is to steal everything good, kill your character, and destroy your life. Then you develop an understanding that anything offered by him leads to death and destruction. Now, the things of God will suddenly replace what you craved in the past.

When true development comes, your responses to life's situations are different. Your trust is different. Your hope is different. Your dreams and aspirations are different. They are aligned with your purpose. You realize that you have a higher calling than where you are now and that God is ready to launch you into a place of wholeness—a place of abundance!

It does not mean that you will not experience pain, hurt, or disappointments, even at this place. However, you must choose faith over reason; you must choose trust over emotions. God is the same yesterday, today, and forevermore, but through development, your perception of God can and will change for the better. Now you are not just looking at Him as God, the Supreme Being and Creator, but now you are also looking at Him as your Father, the one who nurtures and provides and loves unconditionally. You are looking at Him as a multidimensional God who is there for every aspect or situation of your life.

My dad always told the story of a man who died and in death was unaffected by his once familiar surroundings. He said that if you took this man's processional past every place that he had ventured and every person that he had fun with, and past his favorite hangouts, still this man would not get out of the coffin. You could even turn on his favorite music, but he would not get up. He would still lie there. Why? It is because he is dead. To become immune and victorious from those things that held you captive in the past is to allow self to die to your past and surrender to the will of God.

What I am trying to say is that you must keep a direct line open to God at all times. You must get rid of anything that would cause you to become disconnected from the source. There are many resources used in our lives: jobs, finances, and loan or credit power, for instance. But these are only resources. God is the source! And even when the resources are not there, the favor of God can create a way for you. So there is no need to keep revisiting the past and fueling hurts. After all, all you need is in God—the ultimate source! There is no need to get angry with God when you are faced with the challenges of life, but simply align yourself with Him and His purpose for your life.

Even in relationships, you must understand that not everyone who comes into your life is a blessing. Not everyone is sent by God. There are certain relationships that are harmful and abusive. God never intended for anyone to experience physical abuse. No one should live in fear for their life because of the threat of an abuser. God never purposed you to be a punching bag. God never intended for you to have to sleep with one eye open. If you find yourself in a situation like this, get out! Contact the authorities so that they can recommend a local agency. Or contact your church or a local church that teaches the truth of the Word of God and can offer help. Contact family or friends. Usually, for those in such a situation, the abuser tries to keep them in isolation. But there is help! God has provided help for you. Do not become another statistic. You have divine purpose to fulfill!

Then there are verbal abusers. There are those who constantly speak death over others. Parents can do this to their children. Spouses can do this with each other. One who verbally abuses is also one who wants to control. The words are designed to cause others to give up their stance in submission to another's will.

Also, sometimes the words come out of disgust, anger, or frustration. When you see loved ones destroying themselves and on the wrong path, you can feel helpless and then find that verbal abuse has now become a way of communication and expressing your disappointment and pain. There are parents who have labeled their own children as "slow," "worthless," or with other derogatory brandings. They have criticized them negatively in sports and in education. They have said, "You won't amount to anything," or "You'll never be anything!" Words are seeds planted into that individual's life. And harmful words can produce harmful actions if that seed is fertilized and nurtured. Verbal abuse is not the answer.

Examine your life and the words that have been spoken over your life. Have they affected you? Or were you able to shake any negative words off and still walk in who God says that you are? If you have never known what God says about you, then pick up a Bible and read! Why don't you start with John 3:16? It reads, *"For God so loved the world, that He gave His only begotten Son, that whosoever believeth in Him should not perish, but have everlasting life."* Jesus loved you enough to die for your sins. He loved you enough to want to give you abundant life. So do not miss out by embracing those who come to bring death to you.

Parents, embrace your children. Speak life to them. Do not ignore situations or dangers in their lives that you see, but ask God to give you wisdom in how to handle them. Sometimes it may be hard, but God spoke life over you, despite yourself! The pain may be intense right now, but keep pushing. Deliverance is at hand!

Fear (Anxiety of Birth)

In transition, one of the things that can cause you to become lost is the fear of the unknown. You can become fearful or reluctant when you do not have control of the situation or do not understand what is going on. Just as when you trust God during transition and your perception of God changes for the better, if you are lost in the transition, your perception of God changes for the worse. The same God that you boasted about and praised and worshiped is now one that you feel has betrayed you.

If you get to this point and yield to the voice of darkness, then you really do not know God like you thought you knew Him. If you really know Him, although your flesh may feel like this, your spirit man will rise in strength to remind you of God's power and Satan's deceptive ways. God is faithful! He is faithful in getting you to walk in divine purpose so that you can experience all the benefits of the kingdom.

Yes, to feel frustrated or angry, to feel uncertainty at times, can be a natural human reaction during a crisis. You do not need to feel guilty about tears. But you do not have to stay there! To accept the influence of your mind when it speaks defeat coupled with a gamut of emotions and uncertainty is detrimental to your existence. If you really understand who God is, you will understand that He wants what is best for you. No matter what oppositions arise, God can turn it around for your good and make you more than a conqueror.

Your ways are not God's ways, and His thoughts are higher than your thoughts (Isa. 55:8–9). This means that you will not understand everything about God. And you will not always understand why He allows you to go through some of the situations that He allows you to go through sometimes. But know that His plan for your life is greater than what you can ever ask, imagine, or think (Eph. 3:20).

Do not get lost in the transition and begin cursing God instead of blessing Him. Really, during your time of labor and in the midst of your fight and great pain, you should say, "God, I praise You for the new! I bless You for the new mind, new development, new growth, greater spiritual walk, and greater depths in You."

You should praise Him for the greater understanding of who He is, which helps you know more about who you are in Him. You should uplift Him and say, "God, I praise You for where You are taking me. God, I bless You for equipping me to handle new blessings that will soon manifest."

You should glorify God for sending the Comforter, the Holy Spirit, who will lead you and guide you into all truth. You should thank God for fortifying you to go through so that you can benefit from the blessing of victory. Even through pains of labor, you can yet trust God!

There is a process to development. Understand that when an animal dies in the wild, his carcass erodes and fertilizes the very soil that he came from. The soil is then enriched, which causes growth for the flowers, trees, and grass. Then the animals stop by and feed on what has grown. This continues until another animal dies and the cycle is repeated.

There is a life cycle in your walk that causes birth, growth, development, and death . . . birth, growth, development and death . . . for each dimension of your relationship with God, as well as for your life in general. When you have outgrown the place that you are in, God then transitions you into newness.

Through the process of death, there is a weeping season. But you will not stay there. There is life after death when you follow the plan and order of God. There must be death in order to have life. Jesus had to die in order to be resurrected so that we could have life. The covenant was not complete until He was resurrected. It did not end at His death.

So you are not complete until you rise from your ashes—until you are resurrected! You are not complete until you are made whole!

God is a God of strategy and order, in order to accomplish His purpose and bring forth all that He has placed inside of you.

Do not be discouraged as you try to see the manifestation of growth but see only pain. You do not see your children grow from centimeter to centimeter, but they are yet growing. Before you know it, they need new shoes and clothes to accommodate their growth. This is how you grow—step by step, situation by situation, and victory by victory. Even your failures can help you grow. Then before you know it, you are at a new place, equipped with newness in order to operate and succeed in this new area of growth.

Understand that spirituality and growth does not necessarily mean development. This is why both are emphasized in this book. One can grow but never develop. There are children who are born with certain birth defects. The reason is that while they were growing in various stages, something vital was yet missing or lacking from their developmental process. If you miss out on any part of what God allows you to go through, then during the developmental process, you will lack a vital part of fortified sustenance needed for your next situation or challenge in life. How can you miss out? It is by running away from the test, by avoiding the test, by incompletion of the test, by disobedience or by living through the dictates of the flesh, to name a few ways.

Development is the actual expansion of the growth that encompasses depth and dimensions. It is the intricate aspect of growth that delves into every fiber of your being in order to equip you for life—spirit, soul, and body. It is the enabling ability to take what you have learned and that which has caused you to grow and to expand or increase with it. It is a magnified perception of both God and yourself.

There are those believers who grow in the knowledge of the Word. They may even grow to understand certain aspects of God. They will operate in certain levels of faith. But when it comes to development, they choose to stay in a state of infancy. Their minds never grasp certain spiritual revelations that would deepen their concept of God and His spiritual principles. Their perception is limited to only their current and past experiences.

Your growth will be challenged by life. It is how you handle the challenge that defines development. After you come out of that situation by going through God's way, then development has taken place.

Some people are satisfied with limitations and therefore, never experience fullness of life. They will have faith in God for a job but will not have faith and trust Him to help them own their own business. They will trust Him to take care of them daily but will not expand their faith and trust Him to send them a favored husband or wife. They have creative ability but will not have faith in God to use them to initiate change for their community, church, or world. They will have faith in God to work in ministry but will not have faith to increase in ministry. They will have faith in God for some things but will not have faith for others.

Development expands your mind, your faith, and your vision for your life and the lives of others, as well as for the divine purpose of God. Development plunges you into immeasurable depths of relationship and intimacy with God, with positive life-changing results.

There are churches that are stagnant simply because the leader does not have the faith to carry out the vision that God gave him or her. There are people who are at the same place that they were ten and twenty years ago! And they are content. They have embraced mediocrity. But it is an exciting thing to allow God to develop you and to challenge you to expansion despite pain. Then when you experience the victory, you realize that it was worth it all!

So while you are in labor, push! Push hard! Push past the pain! Push past your emotions! Push past what your flesh and mind are telling you! Push through to praise! Do you know what happens when you do not praise? You wave a white flag in the face of the enemy that says, "I surrender to you." When you do not praise, you accept defeat. When you do not praise, you give the enemy honor. When you do not praise, your life declares that you have accepted the words of defeat over the Word of God. So push your way to promise! Each contraction or situation of pain brings you closer and closer to that birth or manifestation of your blessings and destined purpose. And after that last greatest pain, know that the manifestation is next!

You must make a conscious decision that in your current situation, you have come too far to stop trusting God now. Understand that fear opposes faith. You have got to see this through! The blessings and promises are too great for you to try to reason your way through this. Allow God to transition you into greatness.

Because you are moving from familiar to unfamiliar territory, it is uncomfortable. The land is new. The location where you are going is new. There is some fear and apprehension. You are afraid of loss. You are afraid of missing out because of what you see in front of you. But understand that nothing you have, nothing you have experienced, can compare to what God has in store for you! Remember, it is impossible for God to lie (Heb. 6:18).

Birth

During natural birth, the contractions that cause the pain are actually pushing the baby through the birthing canal. The body goes through a cycle of contracting and releasing, contracting and releasing. It grabs and pushes, grabs and pushes. And this process continues to bring that baby from a place that can no longer hold it to a place of endless expansion.

The womb is designed to carry that child for nine months. After that time, the body understands that now is the time to push. Even spiritually, you will sense that now is the time. When the doctor says, "Just one more push," the mother can muster up the strength from somewhere, all in anticipation that this is it—one more step and it is over. Spiritually, you grab hold of faith through the Word and push. Grab hold of faith and push—past pain!

Also, it is the time to praise God as never before. You sense that it is the time for the promise to manifest—now praise God! Praise helps you focus on God's awesomeness. Praise helps you focus on His promises, His strength, and His encouragement. Praise helps you to remember what He has already done, realizing that if He did it before, He will do it again. Praise equips you to stand until the manifestation of promise. Praise crushes and annihilates fear!

In knowing that now is the time for your manifestation of blessings, praise and push! In understanding that this is the appointed time for you to experience the promise, praise and push! In realizing that you have suffered and now is the time of your release, praise and push! Now is the time to stay focused and not get lost in the transition from the old to the new. Your pain has provided you a way out. This birth represents a new life, culminating from all the seeds that you have sown. And now, it is harvest time!

CHAPTER 6

CHASING THE HEART OF GOD

B efore, during, and after the transition, it is crucial to understand
the power and importance of prayer. There are those who tend
to think that prayer is only petitioning God. People generally will
not hesitate to ask God for the things that they want or need. And He
does invite us to.

Then, there is the prayer of petition. The Bible says, *"Ask and it
shall be given. Seek and ye shall find. Knock and the door shall be
opened to you"* (Matt. 7:7). In Mark 11:23–26, there is a mandate to
forgive before your prayers can be answered: *"And when ye stand
praying, forgive, if ye have ought against any: that your Father
also which is in heaven may forgive you your trespasses. But if ye
do not forgive, neither will your Father which is in heaven forgive
your trespasses."* So you can ask anything of our Father as you pray
according to His will. But first you must forgive those who have
brought offenses against you.

People will wonder why their prayers remain unanswered, but
the Bible does stipulate that you must have forgiveness in your
heart. This is why it is so important to let go and follow God over
flesh. When your heart has forgiven, then you have a direct line
or opportunity and privilege to ask of God. *"For verily I say unto
you, that whosoever shall say unto this mountain, Be thou removed,
and be thou cast into the sea; and shall not doubt in his heart, but
shall believe that those things which he saith shall come to pass;*

he shall have whatsoever he saith. Therefore I say unto you, what things soever ye desire, when ye pray, believe that ye receive them, and ye shall have them" (Mark 11:23, 24).

The prayer of petition, or asking of God, is one type of communication with God. In addition, we are to pray the prayer of thanks toward God. The Bible admonishes us to consistently give thanks: *"In every thing give thanks: for this is the will of God in Christ Jesus concerning you"* (1 Thess. 5:18). In every situation, we are to thank God because He is God and the final authority over every situation that we surrender to Him. We thank God even if we do not agree with or understand His will. We thank God in advance, as we believe that His Word is unfailing for our lives. We are to appreciate the Lord and all that He has done for us and even for what He is going to do: *"O give thanks unto the LORD; call upon his name: make known his deeds among the people"* (Ps. 105:1). You show God love with your praise and thanksgiving.

In addition to the prayer of petition and prayers of thanks, most people leave out prayers of intimacy. This is the time that you take just to adore God. So many will voice their requests and perhaps even give thanks for what God has blessed them with, but then their prayer time is over. Generally, people tend to stay away from the Holy of Holies. This is a place where you develop intimacy with God. This is the prayer in which you lose yourself in God. This is the prayer that takes you to the heart of God.

Worship is an intimate experience and a true extension of yourself toward God. In worship, there is an extension of your heart moving from *your* wants and needs to adoration and love toward God. Worship surpasses *you.* Worship is the prayer in which you are focused on God and not yourself. This is the prayer that causes you to extend past your problems and pain and still tell God how wonderful He is. This is the prayer that causes you to bow your heart to Him despite your emotions and tell Him how much you love Him and how great and unfailing He is.

In the Holy of Holies, you adore God, not because of what He has given you, but simply because He is an awesome God and you recognize and appreciate His love, goodness, and power for you. *"Great is the LORD, and greatly to be praised in the city of our God, in the mountain of his holiness"* (Ps. 48:1). *"For I know that the* LORD *is great, and that our Lord is above all gods"* (Ps. 135:5). *"O* LORD *our Lord, how excellent is thy name in all the earth"* (Ps. 8:9).

In the Holy of Holies, there is an uncovering, or unveiling, of yourself the more you honor, love, and adore God. An onion is wrapped in its own skin, and not until it is peeled layer by layer is the true essence of power revealed. Also, in worship, you will begin to see your true self. In worship, you will see just how flawed you are in comparison to God's greatness. In seeing yourself, you will begin to open yourself and move closer to God as your frailties are revealed. In worship you will begin to understand your strengths and limitations.

In worship, you will yield to the direction and plan of God for your life, despite unexpected situations and unwanted pain. Why? Because here you begin to see the Word come alive in your life. Here you stand on the fact that no matter what comes against you, if God be for you, who can be against you (Rom. 8:31). As you adore and magnify God in worship, you will find that your life will be enlarged.

But to get to the Holy of Holies takes a heart that chases after God. It takes a heart of submission to God. It takes a determination that nothing is going to keep you from God. To get to the Holy of Holies takes a true heart that puts God first.

Worship is a heart of love and adoration to God. It is a heart without hidden agendas or motives. The Bible says, *"They that worship God must worship Him in spirit* [not the flesh] *and in truth* [based on the Word of God and not worldly principles]" (John 4:24).

There are those who say, "It does not take all of that." They do not feel that it is necessary to have a consistent prayer life, to fast in order to keep the flesh disciplined, and to read the Word and live it in order to be in the will of God and receive His benefits. Or there are some who will do all of this; however, they do it with the wrong heart, which nullifies their sacrifices.

Doing what God requires in all of this is a form of worship unto God. Worship is not just consecrating, but it is a demonstration of living a consecrated life! Some will say, "It doesn't take all of that."

Yet these are some of the same people who, if they did something nice for you, something that they were excited about and something they went out of their way for but you never acknowledged their actions, would be hurt, angry, and offended. Now we know that when we give, we are supposed to give from our hearts and not expect anything in return. But showing appreciation and proper acknowledgment is an expected response to a kind gesture. So how much more do we owe God? And with adoration and appreciation toward God, we will reap continual benefits!

We were created to worship. God's grace and mercy are extended to us daily. His angels protect us daily. He blesses us to come home to our families daily. Even when the time comes and God calls us home, He has a wonderful place prepared just for us, where there is no more suffering and pain, a place where we will have eternal joy and peace. So we get the best of both worlds as a son or daughter of God.

Worshiping God and moving into the Holy of Holies comes only when the mind, intellect, and reasoning submit to the Spirit of God. In other words, the state of your heart determines whether you will ever obtain the privilege of entering into the Holy of Holies. Isn't it amazing that we can be flawed, but because of a pure heart and love for God, we can still move into the Holy of Holies? We are yet human and will make some mistakes, but thank God that He can see our hearts!

Yes, you will find those who imitate true worship with the uplifting of their hands or the words they utter. However, only those worshiping in Spirit and in truth shall actually enter into the deepest, most intimate place of worship and touch the very heart of God. God said that He is seeking true worshipers. So, if He specifically says "true" worshiper, then there must be "false" worshipers, who care more about their appearance to man than to God.

In the Old Testament during one period of history, the tabernacle was the place of worship for the Israelites. In the tabernacle, you would find the outer court, which is representative of the world. Further in, you would find the Holy Place, which symbolizes the church's separation from the world (outer court). It symbolizes the acceptance of Christ's sacrifice for redemption and salvation.

Additionally, this can be relative to those who have accepted Christ and experienced personal manifestations of His glory.

Before going into the Holy Place, the priests would wash their hands and feet as a symbol of cleansing. Symbolically, this represents the cleansing that was done through Christ's death, burial, and resurrection in the New Testament. Today, through your prayers, you are able to enter into the Holy Place and commune with God. Nevertheless, the Holy Place was not the final destination to experience the most intricate and compelling glory of God.

In the Holy Place, there was a veil that separated the Holy Place from the Most Holy Place. The Most Holy Place represents the habitation of God's glory. When Jesus died on the cross, the veil was torn in two. This exposed the mercy seat and today provides you with direct access to God.

The Most Holy Place represents the liberty of true relationship with God. This is the place where you move from religion to relationship. This is the place where you have a glimpse of heaven. This is the Holy of Holies! In your prayer and time of fellowship, do not stop at the Holy Place, but press past into the Holy of Holies. Allow your spirit to be one with the Spirit of God, and experience His magnificent glory!

You must develop an intimate relationship with God, which provides direction for your life. You must talk to God. In any intimate relationship, there must be communication. This is to say, there must be conversation between both parties. So talk to God. Let Him know how you feel about Him. Then just stay in His presence. Wait for God to speak to you. What has He placed in your heart during your time of worship? Even after being in His presence in prayer and worship and then moving on with your daily life, you still need to listen to your heart as it is directed by God. Worship causes you to love what God loves and hate what He hates. Worship causes your life to truly be in the image of God.

When you come to a place of realization in knowing the true awesomeness of God, then your own life comes into perspective. You no longer look at your life as a random occurrence, but you begin to sense that you are here for a purpose. Regardless of how you got here, God honors the fact that you are here!

As you stay more in the Word of God and in the presence of God, you realize that your survival is truly in staying connected to the source. You realize that God is your real source of peace, strength, encouragement, power, and life. You realize that it is truly imperative to always stay connected to the vine. In John 15:1-9, Jesus lets us know that He is the vine and that anything connected to Him will prosper. Also, from Genesis to Revelation, you realize that all the benefits of life are connected to the benefits of the kingdom of God through Jesus Christ.

When you have experienced the true glory of God, there is nothing else comparable to it. As you become more and more saturated by the glory of God, you know that being in His presence is the ultimate experience of oneness with Him in this human body. You can never get enough of His glory! You are left filled and satisfied, yet still longing and thirsting for more and more of God.

When your desire is to chase after the heart of God, it can sometimes leave you estranged from others in your church or home. When you have put God first and really desire His will, do not think that everyone is going to join in your enthusiasm. You may start to seem strange or peculiar to them. They cannot understand why your conversation doesn't warrant running down another person. They cannot understand why you despise the games that go on in the church world (but not with those who truly walk in the kingdom of God)—games of competition, jealousy, control, and intimidation. They cannot understand why you will not join in.

But you just continue to chase after the heart of God and through every ultimate experience with God. He will reveal more and more of Himself to you. Most of the time, seeing someone so genuine and pure is so rare that when the norm meets the unique, others really do not know how to handle you!

When you chase after the heart of God, sometimes after being right in the midst of other brothers and sisters in the church, you may walk away grieved because even though they just left the presence of the Lord, they can yet backbite and sow seeds of discord. People may begin to say that you think you are better than they are. But do not get upset. Continue to just be unique in the Lord—one of the chosen.

I heard someone once say that the reason why the burning bush got Moses' attention was not just because it was burning, but because it was different from the others. It stood out from the norm! Some people are satisfied with just a touch from God. But you desire real intimacy with God. Countless people will accept God as their Savior but will never allow Him to be their Lord—to reign and rule in *every* area of their lives. Then they cannot handle it when others genuinely allow Him to be Lord of their lives.

I remember crying out to God and asking Him to send people into my life who understood my call, who understood the anointing in my life. I remember crying out, "Lord, please put people in my life who love You first." I remember praying and crying and asking God to put people in my life who were not in ministry for show, entertainment, or for the purpose of proving something. But I asked Him to send people into my life who genuinely loved God and souls. And, He has been doing just that. Without love . . . all that we do is in vain, as sounding brass and tinkling symbols (1 Cor. 13:1). There are those who go through the routine of religion and never experience or even lead the people into relationship. When you truly chase after the heart of God, your goal is not to desecrate the life of another. Your goal is to help build. This is a true sign of your heart. You will not seek to defend yourself, knowing that God will do it for you.

In my observations and experiences, I have seen Christians who attend church on Sundays and during the week, participate in various areas of ministry, and pray and fast, but who yet remain at a level of immaturity. When all these things have become mere routine, just something to do, then you can habitually do the right thing but never experience true growth and spiritual maturity in it.

Why? How? It is because the motive of the heart is wrong. The focus is off God and more on the title and position, more on the gift or talent, more on the delivery to impress, rather than on allowing God to use you to bring about change. Or it can result from the acceptance of mediocrity and the willingness to limit God in your life. It can be that your mind has never expanded from the time that you first accepted the Lord into your life.

Also, it is a very uncomfortable feeling to mature and leave friends and loved ones behind. All of a sudden, just as you might seem strange to them, they seem foreign and strange to you. Then you come to a place that you recognize that where they are now is where you used to be. You also accept the fact that here is now where you are, and you enjoy the ride! There is still a place even greater that you need to go.

There are those leaders who are content with using clichés to get a reaction from the people. Then what you find are some church-goers who base their entire experience with God on whether the preacher tantalized their emotions. Also, I have seen countless churches filled with nonbelievers who are on their rolls, who have become so complacent with just coming to church. They do not even consider change. Why? It is because there is no anointing to convict, only mere emotionalism.

There are some who have perceived the pulpit as a throne, rather than a place of true divine leadership for God's heritage. There is so much pride and arrogance in the pulpit that the people no longer respect the call as God designed it, but rather see it as a celebrity status or a get-rich-quick business. All the while, sincere hearts are dying because they have never known God the way that He wants them to.

God is also bringing leadership into accountability. He is raising up those after His heart and pulling down, as well as exposing, deception and hypocrisy. I hear ministries blaming the people for seeking out true leaders after the heart of God. And certainly, you will always have a share who will church hop. However, we as leaders must also take inventory of ourselves!

God's heritage is also looking for leaders who saturate them-selves in prayer and worship and live according to God's spiritual standards. God's heritage is looking for leaders who understand that each child is different and will not play one against the other, leaders who do not have attitudes such as "Okay, if this one will not be at my disposal at all times, then I will promote the other over him." God's heritage is looking for leaders who care about the people and not leaders whose primary concern is what they can take from them.

I am not talking about leaders seeking those who are faithful and committed. I am talking about leaders who are looking to control. Leaders, it is highly unlikely that you will ever have 100 percent favorability in your congregation. However, just be sure that your life lines up with the Word of God. It is imperative for leaders to keep their ears to the mouth of God and chase after the heart of God. Accountability!

People of God, God needs true worshipers! Make no mistake about it—true worshipers of God will still experience temptations and tests. They will still get upset or angry at times. They will still see and experience disappointments sometimes. But because of the experience of true intimacy with God, the love they have for God will cause them to yield to the will of God.

Reach for God! Fight to stay in His presence. Allow Him to saturate you with His glory. Allow Him to speak to you, lead you, comfort you, direct you, and impart more of His Spirit into your life. You will find that some people will not humble themselves to this place. And this is why those who will are those who stand out among many. This is not intentional. This is not their goal. But the extreme anointing is a light that shines so brightly that it just cannot be hidden.

When you stay in the face of God, chasing after His heart, you will never have to worry about being overlooked or stepped on, because ultimately the anointing will open those doors for you. The anointing will take you places that the flesh cannot go. The anointing will crush the head of the enemy and destroy anything that would try to block the way God has set before you.

Your love for God should supersede everything. This love for Him will enable the other areas of your life (attitude, peace, success) to be put into perspective because all that you do will be based on His character of love. There are those who profess God but in actuality have placed Him on a back burner. In other words, they turn to Him only when they need something.

My constant prayer is always to acknowledge God for His leadership and direction. And my prayer is "More of You, Lord...less of me." My prayer and heart's desire is for the perfect will of God. These prayers are earnest because I do not want to become what I have seen and what God despises, an abuser of His heritage, His people. When you chase after God as a deer panteth for the water (Ps. 42:1), it is as if you are saying, "Just like I cannot live without air or water, I cannot not live without You, Lord."

CHAPTER 7

THE DANGERS OF NOT LETTING GO

⌒⌒

L etting go is sometimes one of the hardest things to do. Whether it is letting go of a relationship, job, idea, philosophy, obsession, addiction, or anything else, it can be challenging, but it is an obtainable goal. You can become so dependent upon a thing or entity that it can drive you into a place of comfort, complacency, or eternal dependence. Who really likes to leave their comfort zone? But anytime you wrap yourself around something so tightly that you cannot move or grow, you close the door of opportunity, even for God.

It is easy to promote letting go when it refers to an obvious addiction or obsession. Of course, the visible consequences can show anyone that it is not healthy, but destructive. However, what about those things that can gradually cause you to deteriorate naturally or spiritually, emotionally, or intellectually? What about those things that seemed like just a taste at first but years later have become cravings and crippling devices in your life? Why? It is because when you had a chance to let go, you would not.

In the natural, think about those with a job opportunity that came along. This was an opportunity that one had desired and been waiting for. He wanted to move to another job, yet when given the opportunity, he made all kinds of excuses not to take the necessary steps to transition to the new. Without wavering, he chose to stay at a place where he was unhappy and had no chance of advancement.

The decision was not based on any direction from God or even on natural necessity, but simply the desire to not have to get used to another company, as well as on fear: "What if they have a layoff right after I am hired?" The decision was not based on the desire to retire from where he was or for fear of losing seniority, but merely on not wanting to go through the inconvenience of change. So he remained unhappy where he was.

When the desire to move forward is outweighed by the desire to remain, you will always find yourself stagnant and frustrated. You may even open yourself to unhealthy relationships simply to relieve frustration. In this scenario, the same opportunity could come to another person who chooses to move forward and in time experiences elevation and success, while the one who chose to remain simply experiences more unhappiness and bitterness.

When I think about the last fifteen years of my life, I find that there are still some questions in my mind as to what happened concerning certain relationships and certain people. What happens when you open your heart to give of yourself in friendship and love only to find out years later that the relationship has changed? Automatically, one may assume that some kind of difference caused a severing. But this is not necessarily true. It can be true in some cases, yet not true in others.

For those instances when you find yourself longing for that voice or those words of comfort that are no longer there, you may wonder, "What happened?" You may question what you said or did or even should have said or done. In some cases, you may still have contact, but you know that the relationship has changed. You may still genuinely love each other, but the relationship has changed.

Then there are those relationships that are actually completely severed. Sometimes people disappear from your life, and you just never know why. Many times it is because of transition and the place that you are now going. It may not have been a conscious decision, but you just wake up one day to find that your relationships have changed. You may long for the former, but you have to come to grips with the fact that there is a transition in your life. Some transitions are so much more beneficial to you than you realize. If we all knew the entire benefit of transition, we would not despise change but would embrace it.

In my experiences, I have found that I want to hold on for dear life to friendships and those who have blessed and inspired me. But I have also found that there are those who come into your life throughout the years and although you may desperately want them to stay, that does not always happen. I find that friends who lent you their ears at one time may be around only for a season. I have found that those precious jewels who pray and encourage you through your hurts, pains, and disappointments may be allowed to do so only for a while. The transition of change brings about many emotions and experiences. What once was is no longer. But it is your attitude toward change that really establishes you.

One transition of change that seems to be a problem for many people is the change from the past to the future. Countless people have left their lives in the past and will never experience all the wonders that await them until they have a mind to let go and move on. I am in no way saying that you are to forget your past entirely, because in order to grab hold of your future, you must understand your past. In other words, understand and be aware of where you came from in order to know where you are going. Considering your experiences of the past will serve to enhance your future. Understanding your past will help you embrace your future.

Some of the painful moments from your past may have come about simply because you made the wrong decisions and perhaps were involved with the wrong people. It is important to acknowledge God in everything and allow Him to direct your path. It is important to know why people come into your life. Are they sent by God to enhance your life? Or are they sent by Satan to destroy it? Or are they in your life for a season or for a permanent and long-lasting friendship? It is also important not to forget your past so that you will not repeat the same errors and remain caught in an endless cycle of failure and disappointment in the present and future. When you rewind and take a glimpse at your past, you are able to see progress, growth, and success, as well as failure and disappointment. In all probability, you will see a combination of both. We all have had some type of failure in our lives. However, if you quit because of failures, then your past will reflect years of emptiness, void, confusion, and a life of no substance, which will filter into your present and future. You will exemplify a life without hope.

But Jesus Christ came to give hope because He is the hope of glory. It is amazing, but the power of the Lord in your life will remove those negative thoughts, even about yourself, and replace them with a winning attitude. That is the key for success—a renewed mind, which will bring about a winning attitude. He will lead you and guide you into purpose and destiny. He will help you pull your life into a place of victory and testimony, rather than failure and regret.

In my lifetime, I have encountered countless people who are stuck in their past. Ten, fifteen, twenty, or even twenty-five years ago, they were at the same place in their lives, or perhaps a better place then, than they currently are in. I am not specifically talking about only nonbelievers. Many are believers! They have lived with no aspirations, dreams, or hope. Their words speak defeat, their minds think defeat, and their lives demonstrate defeat and complacency. I often say how sad it is to profess Christianity and yet live a defeated life on this earth.

When my extended family gets together, whether spontaneously or planned, we always have a great time. During those gatherings, at one point or another, we are going to reminisce. Then we all find ourselves roaring with laughter! That kind of reminiscing is fun and healthy. The Bible says that *"a merry heart* [laughter] *doeth good like a medicine"* (Prov. 17:22). This is to say, laughter is good medicine. Remembering great times is fun. However, going back to that moment is much different from embracing your past as your current lifestyle.

Sadly, there are those who still live in the past. Their hearts and minds have become enslaved to the past. There should be a time in your life when you have grown and matured naturally, intellectually, emotionally, and spiritually. But when you see the same people living in the same place for years, there is something wrong in the growth and development process. Anytime your greatest experiences are in the past only, there is something wrong. Anytime the most joy you have experienced in life is in the past, then you need a change in your life.

Here, I offer you Jesus! When your entire conversation is consistently based on reminiscing about what you used to do, then it is time for self-examination. What about what you are doing now and what you will do? It is time for a change!

There is a danger in not letting go when it is time. The danger is that the past and future are never to meet. You cannot see Monday while it is Tuesday. Six in the morning will never meet with six in the evening in the same time zone. There are some things that will never walk hand in hand.

In your life, in order to move forward, you will have to let go of some things that can never go hand in hand with your future. Some things or people will not be allowed to stay connected to you as you move from the past to the present and future. Your mind-set must be elevated to the future. Your heart must beat to the rhythm of the future. Your talk must echo the vision of the future.

Some of those so-called friends who have held you captive because of loyalty cannot go into the future. Some relationships with friends may sever because they are not interested in going into the new. A true friend will allow you to be who God created you to be. A true friend will not hold you hostage to what he or she did for you in the past. A true friend will help you move into the future. And a true friend will know when it is time to let go as your crutch so that you will be able to stand on your own for the future.

If you do not let go but remain enslaved to your past by the voice of the enemy who loves to say, "Remember when . . .," you will never experience true liberation. He absolutely loves to keep you a prisoner to failures, broken relationships, bad decisions, addictions, or anything else that caused bondage in your life. He loves to show you who you perhaps were and not allow you to see who God ordained you to be. But by the renewing of your mind through the Word of God, you will know that it is just a deceptive device used to keep you from going where you are destined to go.

Some people fear letting go. They fear loneliness. They fear failure. They cannot comprehend the love that God has and the blessings that He has waiting for them. They cannot even see the future because of the fear that clouds their lives.

Some women will not let go of that abuser because they fear that they will be alone. Then they determine, "He's better than nothing." Instead, a renewed mind will say, "I am better than this! God created me for purpose, and being abused is not my calling." They will realize that anything designed to tear them down is not of God.

God is a planter and builder. He orchestrates our lives as we acknowledge Him to direct our paths. Then as we yield to His leading, our lives become a fine symphony perfectly orchestrated in a harmonic flow. The ultimate danger of not letting go is that you will miss out on the wonderful, abundant life that God has planned for you and your seed.

If you are not a believer, you can start letting go simply by accepting the Lord Jesus Christ into your life. Why don't you join His royal family today! Pray this prayer:

PRAYER: Father God, please forgive me from all my sins. I am a sinner, and I repent for every deed done in my life that was not in accordance with Your Word and Your purpose for my life. I do believe that Jesus Christ is the Son of God. I do believe that Your Son, Jesus, has died for my sins. I do believe that He was resurrected from the grave and that He rose up from the grave with all power. Today I accept You, Lord Jesus, into my life. I receive Your newness. I receive Your wholeness, and I receive the Word of God as my divine instruction to live an abundant life in this present world and in the world to come. Amen.

Romans 10:9–10:

"That if thou shalt confess with thy mouth the Lord Jesus, and shalt believe in thine heart that God hath raised him from the dead, thou shalt be saved. For with the heart man believeth unto righteousness; and with the mouth confession is made unto salvation."

Romans 10:9–10 AMP:

"Because if you acknowledge and confess with your lips that Jesus is Lord and in your heart believe (adhere to, trust in, and rely on the truth) that God raised Him from the dead, you will be saved. For with the heart a person believes (adheres to, trusts in, and relies on Christ) and so is justified (declared righteous, acceptable to God), and with the mouth he confesses (declares openly and speaks out freely his faith) and confirms [his] salvation."

I do admonish you to join a Spirit-filled church that is based on the Word of God. The fellowship will strengthen you as you learn and grow. The Word and worship will continuously build you.

If you are a believer, you can pray this prayer as a step of faith in letting go of your past and moving forward into the future:

PRAYER: Father God, today I take this step in trusting You more than ever for my life. There are some things that have held me captive in my mind, my emotions, and even my body, but today I release everything to You. I release (begin naming those things that you need to *let go of*), and I will commit myself to reading Your Word daily and renewing my mind. Through faith, I will have understanding and will be strengthened daily through Your Word. Your strength will help me to resist temptations that held me in bondage in the past or those that may come in the future. I confess that the very thing (call it out) that enslaved me in the past, I now have victory over because You have provided me with power through the Holy Spirit. I commit to a dedicated prayer life in order to obtain and maintain wholeness in You. I confess, according to Your Word, that I have the mind of Christ. In Jesus' name, amen.

Let this day be a day of newness for your life!

CHAPTER 8

THE ROOT OF BITTERNESS

There are three types of battles defined in literature that I would like to use to illustrate the point of bitterness and how it can take root. Painful situations can result in the manifestation of bitterness in every area of your life, if you allow it. Bitterness is a foul spirit that festers from the heart and spreads throughout your being—spirit, soul, and often body—until it eats you from the inside out. It attacks those it comes into contact with and can be contagious to those who accept it.

Have you ever seen someone who has allowed bitterness to have full reign in his or her life? It is ugly! Bitterness never starts out by waving a flag and announcing its arrival. Instead, bitterness enters in as a small seed, but as it continues to feed off the anger and hurts of your life that you constantly rehearse in your mind or conversation, it grows into a deadly poison. It infiltrates through your mind and flows down through your heart and is displayed in your life.

Oftentimes you may find yourself in a battle of "who I really am" versus "who I am perceived to be." It is not always comfortable to deal with who you really are. It seems easier to deal with who you are perceived to be than to deal with your true self. This is because many people adorn themselves in facades with hopes of making an impression on others. Many live their lives in anticipation of what another person may think.

The perception of others can sometimes be so far from who you really are that it is embarrassing, if you happen to be an honest person. I remember when I was in my early to mid-twenties and was going through some tests when one of the sisters in the Lord called. She was a friend about my age. We talked for a while. During the conversation, I began to try to encourage her to let her know that we all get tired sometimes. As I recall, I had been trying to encourage her to wait on God and not make certain decisions on her own. I let her know that everyone has issues that confront them. Not until she said, "Not you. You? Not you!" did I realize that she had never, ever dreamed that I could get discouraged or go through anything negative. This was astonishing to me.

She actually confirmed this with her mouth. She perceived me as a rock at all times. She thought that my life was continuously a bed of ease. I simply could not believe that a person could be that naïve. But she really could not believe that I sometimes got discouraged too.

I began to tell her that everyone needs encouragement…everyone goes through challenges. Everyone experiences hurts or pains in life. But she was really shocked. Then, she heard in my voice that there were times when I had actually gotten weary too, as I continued to share some testimonies. But I had made the decision to yet trust God.

At that point, I began to ponder the realization that the perception others may have of you is not always accurate. You must be true to yourself. Your life should not be governed by perception and façades. The battle between reality and perception within is waged in various areas: your thoughts, your dreams, your emotions. I believe that if we were able to read minds, we would all walk around aghast at some of the thoughts and dreams that emanate through seemingly the most spiritual of people.

The enemy enjoys launching his attacks to cause you to question who you are. But the victory will come only if you deal with the issues that would stop you from becoming who you are destined to become. There are real inner struggles for some. You may struggle with your identity because you never knew your mother or father. You may struggle with your abilities because of the negative words of death spoken over your life. You may struggle with fear and failure because of generational curses in your bloodline. You may struggle with standing on your own two feet because of abuse. You may struggle with things you have done in your past. You may struggle with choices you have made in the past. But God has a remedy—His healing power!

In your situation, God can heal and deliver. Then your misery will become your launching pad to victory; the very thing that tried to hold you captive, you will now be a victor over, as well as become able to help others versus becoming a carrier of bitterness. But how can this be? It can happen by first being real with yourself and real with God. So you do have a choice!

Bitterness snatches your life away slowly but surely. Bitterness holds you prisoner to your hurt and pain. Bitterness never allows you to experience true peace. So you live under a guise of false peace. But you always have to deal with the true reality as you go home at night with those negative thoughts and feelings of anger, hurt, disappointment, betrayal, oppression, or depression. Bitterness is a sure way that Satan has to ensure that you never receive the fullness of life that God has for you. Now let us examine the tracks of bitterness.

Man Versus Man

There are always confrontations when you are trying to move forward, as we previously stated. Anytime you try to do good, evil will always be present. There are those who give themselves over to evil, as we discussed in previous chapters. They have become ambassadors of evil for the kingdom of darkness.

Sometimes the attacks come from those you least expect. But you must understand that if you are anointed, you are a magnet for attacks. If you walk in God's favor, attacks will come. In the natural, there are those who do not want to take the steps necessary to become victorious and successful. They want a microwave change. When that does not happen and they see your success, they resent you.

There are some who do not want to go through what it takes for the anointing, which is the empowering and enabling sanctioning of God. But understand that God's power will always reign supreme.

Those who do not want to do what it takes will become complacent and simply settle for imitating the anointing. Yet they become angry with you for wanting to move forward.

A minister once said to me, "How can anyone take you to a place that they have never been?" This is not referring to those who are in place to point you in the direction that you are called to go. This is directed to those who feel that they and they alone know what is best for your life. God will allow some to be there for you by accepting the vision for your life and being an instrument to help get you to your destined place. Yet, some may not even understand the vision and total purpose assigned to your life. They may applaud and support you reaching one level, but if you move past what they can see for you…into areas they are either uncomfortable or unfamiliar with…then you may be faced with a challenge.

Also, you must understand that some do not want to go where you are heading. They do not want to make the sacrifices needed. Therefore, be prepared, because the spirit of selfishness will not want to willingly allow you to excel. So in life you will experience confrontations or attacks from others, but it has been said that your attitude will determine your altitude, or success.

You may experience something at your job at the very time that you have chosen to move closer to God. Isn't it something how just when you make a deeper commitment, there seems to be something that comes along to try to distract you from moving forward? At the very time that I made a deeper commitment to God, I recall a situation that arose. Through prayer and trust in God, I was victorious and ended up receiving a promotion at work from the trouble. You do not have to worry when things are lost or stolen, because if God has to create doors for you, He will. He created the world; surely, He can create a door for you to be blessed!

During the battle, I had a choice. I could have been manipulative and walk in deception, like others were. I could have become revengeful. I could even have become very bitter, because, after all, the weapon did form. I had to make a choice.

I worked through my frustrations and decided to keep trusting God. I continued to confess the Word of God so that I would not allow my emotions to play right into the enemy's hands. I do not applaud myself, because my flesh was in opposition to everything that I did. Instead, I applaud God who gave me strength to trust Him!

You can allow the Holy Spirit to help you control your emotions. Yes, I was upset because of deception and lies in that work environment. Yes, I had questions as to why things were allowed to happen. But this was a time to trust God, knowing that the power of God would prevail over evil.

I anointed myself and spoke peace, according to the will of God. I continued to stand on the Word of God. I said that I was going to trust God. And when the manifestation of God's blessing took place, there were those who were shocked! I received elevation and was victorious over the plot of the enemy. There are actually some people who really believe that they are the final authority in your life. But God has the last word when you trust Him!

There are those who have experienced broken relationships and have allowed themselves to become bitter because of it. Many of you have decided not to trust again because of this type of pain. So now when God brings someone into your life, you will not accept the blessing. You are so hung up on the wrong that was done to you in the past that you do not even recognize that God has just placed someone in your life who will far exceed what you can ask, imagine, or think. Then there are those who may accept the blessing but then lose it later because they are enslaved to the bitterness of the past. Countless people have experienced the pain and agony of a broken relationship. However, if you continue to carry that with you into a new relationship, it will not last. You have a choice! In understanding who you are and who God created you to be, you can begin to heal. When you understand that God wants you to have joy and happiness in your life, you are more apt to let go of the past, let go of the pain, and let go of the bitterness. He wants you to experience true love, peace, and fulfillment in your life.

So there will be battles with outside sources, but you must know that if you open the door to bitterness, it will cause you to miss out on your blessings. Do not allow others to cause you to choose bitterness. Remember, God is the final authority in your life if you are a believer. And no matter what anyone says or does, he or she cannot stop your blessings. But if you choose to harbor bitterness, hurt, and unforgiveness, then you have sentenced yourself to a life of misery and stopped the flow of your own blessings.

Again, as a reminder, the book of Mark does command that when you pray, first forgive. So many people move outside this principle and yet expect God to do everything for them. The principles of God do not change. These are spiritual principles that God has provided for us to live an abundant life in every area of our lives. And there is no exception to the rule.

Do not fool yourself simply because you may see a blessing here or there. The Bible also says that God rains on the unjust as well as the just. However, there are some blessings that just will not manifest outside other principles of God. And if you are a mature Christian, this is an absolute for you. On the outside, you may fool some of the people some of the time. But rest assured, bitterness will eventually take over your life, and it will be quite evident to everyone else after a while that you are not a whole person.

Know the real enemy. It is not the one who is doing the hurting. This person has accepted the opportunity to be used to attack you. This person has allowed himself to be a vessel raised up against you. And that is someone who is in desperate need of prayer.

So now here is your chance! Even as you pray for the person, you will be healed and stay healed. Let go of the bitterness that has been brought about by others. It is not worth it. The greatest pleasure Satan and anyone used by him will have is for you to fail and become stagnant in your life. Choose to release the pain and bitterness. Ask God to help you as you renew your mind through the Word of God. And soon those hurts of the past and those broken relationships will seem like distant memories, and you will know that God has something better for you. But those experiences and memories will help you realize that it takes only a choice and free will to move forward and break free from bondage.

Man Versus Nature

Man's need to conquer the wild is one aspect of man versus nature. His need to battle the elements is heightened with the aspect of the possibility of conquering. To climb Mount Everest, to swim across massive waters, and to hunt or even camp out in certain areas of the wild are examples of man versus nature. To look at nature and conquer it in some way, no doubt, breeds a posture of either superiority or admiration, especially if no one else or very few have obtained it. Let's look further at the spiritual aspect of man versus nature.

Becoming engaged in any battle is consuming. But it seems that as long as you can isolate the problem with reasoning, the battle seems winnable. If you are dealing with the issues stemming from another person, you have isolated the cause of pain. When you are dealing with yourself, you can recognize that if you yield to change, there is hope to win that battle. However, when the battle is man against nature, it can seem so intense, leaving you feeling helpless, trapped, and internally vulnerable.

This battle is equated to natural elements that man cannot control. As a natural illustration, in literature, a man trying to survive an avalanche is a quest against natural elements. Another case in point of man versus nature is when man has to survive a devastating storm, such as a hurricane or tornado. When a man is confronted by a wolf or bears in a movie and must make effective decisions for his survival while lost in the wild, this is a portrait of man versus nature.

Being confronted with this type of battle can bring a person to the point of true passion or despair. It can bring a person to an apex of strength, determination, and increased will to survive or it can bring a person to the place of throwing up his or her hands in defeat. This type of battle can illuminate your mind with great persever-ance in an effort to survive, live, and not die! Or it can hemorrhage every fragment of hope from your life, as you stare face to face with death.

When opposition comes as an intangible force, it seems like you are fighting elemental forces beyond your reach. When a loved one is sick, seeing him or her suffer can leave you with such a feeling of helplessness. Then you battle with not being able to bring resolution to your loved one's suffering, because you cannot seem to positively effect their situation.

Hurricanes, tsunamis and tornadoes, for instance, can be categorized as intangible and uncontrollable forces...storms. Hurricane Katrina caused severe devastation beyond what anyone could imagine. Although the news reported hurricane winds and brutal rain, most people were still caught off guard with its final crippling effects. It seemed to be far greater than what anyone had ever imagined. The lives of numerous people changed drastically.

To see someone you love going through any crisis or tragedy that seems undeniably out of your scope of assistance can even cause you to feel and carry that person's pain. Even if you battle a situation that seems impossible to win, you are brought to a crossroads of choice: to believe the report of God or to accept the seemingly inevitable. For some, this type of pressure can cause immeasurable emotional devastation without faith and true belief that God is with you no matter what. If you are not cautious and prayerful, it can create a wound so vast that it continuously bleeds frustration and bitterness because your back is against the wall. You never saw this coming, and there is no tangible remedy.

There are some situations that you may face that do not offer a ready solution. You simply must trust God to move forward in life and not remain in suffering. You may even feel that your own survival is predicated upon your bringing some resolution and gaining some type of victory through all that has confronted your loved one.

Man versus nature—those unpredictable occurrences that can leave you feeling trapped, buried, or severely scarred with residue. These are unexpected situations that might not readily offer a tangible solution. They can leave you feeling isolated, as well as socially, emotionally, and psychologically barred from reality. These are those situations where you may have even seen signs, but you never realized the total devastation, such as in Hurricane Katrina.

When they have become reality, situations that overtake you do not have to permanently build a platform of eternal suffering in your heart. Through the agony of why, through the uncertainties of life, through the lack of closure in some cases, you can still make a choice to embrace bitterness and live in your ashes or to reach forward knowing that there are better things to come.

To understand that *you* do not have the power to change some situations is to begin to accept your own healing, as well as release your faith in God. Then you can experience closure from within. Only God can move in the situation to raise you from your ashes. But you do have the power to choose to embrace the change that God will bring.

Man versus Self

Sometimes it seems as if battles are more tangible, as in a battle against another person. But when the battle is man versus self, you have to deal with your own issues and intense struggles. Many people do not want to do this.

In confronting your own issues, you then realize that you are not perfect. You realize that you have failed at one time or another and perhaps even fallen. You realize that there are things in your heart that you have harbored that brought you to a state of suspicion, defense, anger, or bitterness.

If you are honest, you would have to admit that sometimes the greatest battles are from within. (You may want to re-read chapter 3, "The Real Battleground.") If you are a person who cannot be happy when your brother or sister is blessed, that is a sure sign of bitterness, jealousy, insecurity, or other internal issues. You can hide behind a pliable smile, but your actions will eventually betray you and eventually say something different.

People who have trouble with bitterness because they are always comparing themselves to others are like ticking time bombs. All they need is the right fuel to ignite them into acting out their bitterness. I have been blessed, and many have seen elevation in my ministry; however, not everyone is genuinely excited about what God is doing in my life. I have seen people change their countenance when my family walks into a room. I have seen people gravitate to the door to keep from speaking to us. I have seen people do anything and everything to avoid an encounter with us. Yet we have never done anything offensive to them.

I have also seen those who sit and wait for an opportunity to say something offensive to the person or people that they just dislike for no reason. And some of the same ones will stand in the sanctuary and mimic the ushering in of the Spirit of the Lord. There is definite confusion and an obvious battle within their lives.

The problem is that some people allow bitterness, because of their own lives' situations and choices, to become a leading factor in their thought lives and actions. They are bitter because they have made the decision to hold on to their own hurts and failures of the past. Again, you must know when to let go, and when you do, move on! Otherwise, bitterness will be the very thing that defines your life.

A free spirit in the Lord can be genuinely happy for others. A free spirit in the Lord can reach out and help support others. A free spirit in the Lord is not intimidated because of doors that are opening for another. Instead, free spirits can rejoice with you when the manifestations of blessings come to fruition, as they can stand on the promises for their own lives. And free spirits in the Lord do not allow insignificant things to captivate their lives or feed their own self-gratification in the trials of another.

The Word of God is a mirror that projects an image of God. In looking through the mirror, you will be able to see if your image truly reflects your Father. The choice to deny the imperfections and issues only causes delay in your healing, deliverance, and blessings. It causes frustration within your own life when you always push away accountability by blaming another person. Some people still blame their mother for what she did not do. They blame their father for not being there, when in life they have had countless opportunities to grab hold of the positive things that could springboard them into abundant life.

You choose to remain stuck in the blame game. Blaming another is an excuse to avoid dealing with the truth about yourself. Blaming another is an excuse to avoid putting forth the effort to move on. In other words, no matter what another person has done to you, if you choose to move forward in life, you can! But sadly for some of you, in your own mind, it is easier to remain in your ashes than to experience any type of rejection or failure, which could inevitably be used as a learning experience to launch you into a victorious life.

Some believers have even immersed themselves in the masquerade game, hiding their issues week after week behind the religious posture of church attendance or activity. They know what to say. They know what to do. They can mimic the anointing. They grab hold of the latest spiritual or religious language, all in an effort to convince others that God favors them or uses them or that God thinks they are really okay. Yet when they go home, they must deal with the true reality of their own issues. But all along, if they were true to themselves and acknowledged their inner hurts, thoughts, emotions, and struggles to God, they could really be free. But because they choose to avoid the truth about themselves and continually live behind a mask, the bitterness that is constantly growing contaminates them and attempts to seek out and infect others.

Bitterness does not have to hold you captive. It is simply a matter of choice to either be free to experience the benefits of surrendering totally to God or to remain in captivity of mind and emotions and receive final outward manifestations. Bitterness eventually turns into hatred, and hatred destroys the soul and spirit, and through sickness, even the body.

Another internal struggle that keeps you from obtaining is fear. Fear will cripple your life. Fear will keep you in bondage. Fear will keep you locked in restraints as everyone else passes you by and as you see others receive blessings that were promised to you.

When there is a mandate from God for you to walk in a particular gift or calling, but you refuse to or continually back down because of fear, remember that the job still needs to get done. So what is God going to do? He will use someone else.

I remember when I was in the church that I grew up in, God would use me at times to lead devotional songs. You would sit in your seat, and when a song was placed on your heart and if you had an opening during the time of devotion, then you would just start singing your song. I can recall a couple of instances when God placed a particular song on my heart, but because of fear at that particular time (we could have had visitors or prestigious people in our midst), I did not sing it. I would prepare to sing it, but then I would back down. Then after a little while, God would use someone else to sing the same song! And I would see the manifestation of God's glory through that song. It would change the entire atmosphere and usher in the presence of the Lord. After a few times of seeing this, I knew that God had placed that song on another's heart because I had been too fearful to be obedient. I knew that I had just missed my blessing. It was a definite lesson learned.

I grew up in a large family. Therefore, as I was growing up, when I would go out, I was always with my siblings or my parents (at other times, my friends). But after I grew up and moved out, I began to notice that I was very uncomfortable in going out alone. When I was driving, I was uncomfortable knowing that I did not have anyone else in the car to talk with.

I also never liked coming into a service late—first, because I believe in being on time; but second, because I was paranoid about people staring at me. I never liked walking around for the offering, for the same reason. I would admire the young people dancing and praising God in the church, but for years I would not, even though I wanted to so badly. But because of people looking, I would not.

We have a few major highways in the area that I grew up in. However, I would drive primarily on only two: the parkway and Route 1. I felt comfortable driving on those highways because they took me to the mall! Also, the mall was only about twenty minutes away. Then at times, I would travel one other highway, Route 78/24, which took me to another mall about ten to fifteen minutes away. So I limited myself to my comfort zone.

Every now and then, my father would ask me to take a ride with him to see my aunt, and he would ask me to drive. That was a different highway, and I was very uncomfortable. However, knowing that my father was there enabled me to do it.

Fear had stifled my growth and was crippling my life, causing me to know only the environment that I was familiar with. It never allowed me to broaden my horizons and explore what other endless possibilities were beyond my borders. But I thank God for the Holy Spirit!

The Holy Spirit began to work on me as I stayed in the Word. I began to see and understand more about my heavenly Father. In that, I then began to look at myself in comparison to my Father. Remember, if I am created in His image, which I am, then I should reflect His characteristics.

God used my sons to cause me to grow, develop, and mature. I looked at my sons and said that I did not want them to be like I was. I did not want them to be limited to their immediate surroundings. I wanted them to grab hold of every positive opportunity that God brought their way. I wanted them to have the opportunities for unlimited possibilities. In this, I began to expand my mind.

Whenever we were challenged by something that we thought we could not do or achieve, my dad would always say, *"I can do all things through Christ that strengtheneth me"* (Phil. 4:13). Even when we attempted to explain yet again why we felt the way that we did, he would interrupt with, "I can do all things . . ." So I grabbed hold of this Scripture when my sons were invited to a coworker's home over an hour away up a highway that I had never been on except for about ten minutes. They were invited to her son's first birthday party. My boys were one and three at the time. This coworker lived in a very unfamiliar area, almost near the next state, but the directions were very easy. This provoked me to try it.

So I took my sons, money, and phone; filled up with gas; and went on my way. When I got to her house, I was amazed that I had driven all this way with no other adult! We had a wonderful time. I saw her beautiful home and thought, "If God blessed her, He can bless me too." In that one experience alone, God began to broaden my horizons by expanding my mind.

Remember, it just takes a seed! This was the beginning of some of my life's adventures. To some of you, this may seem like a trivial thing. But if you knew the fear that I had back then that was crippling my life, you would understand that this one event was a stepping-stone for God to bring me to the place where I am today.

It may surprise you how a change in one thought can change your life. My change was such that I could go outside my immediate surroundings by myself (with no other adult) and have a life. This sparked my curiosity as the boys were growing up, and now I am no longer in bondage to fear! The Holy Spirit continually reminds me He is in charge of my life. It does not mean that the enemy won't try to bring you back into bondage, but it is up to you whether you will accept it.

I notice that whenever God thrusts me into a new area, fear tries to rear its ugly head again. However, know that what God calls you to do, He equips you to do. Sometimes you may get nervous about new things, which is a natural emotion. But the enemy tries to enlarge it into a crippling fear to cause you to completely turn away from that gift, career, position, ministry, or calling for which God has purposed your life.

Fear also feeds on your own intimidations. Now sometimes you may get intimidated if someone that you admire is in your presence, or if you are in front of an audience that is different from the type of audience that you are used to being in front of, or if you are the center of others' expectations. But this fear can be put under subjection through the power of the Holy Spirit, who enables you to carry out that which He has purposed for you to do. You can make the decision that nervous situations that can be intimidating will not be heightened to actual fear.

Conquering certain fears and intimidations can be a simple matter of perspective. My fear of moving outside my immediate surroundings was apparently a fear of being alone, insecurity in my abilities to reach my destination driving alone, insecurity in myself and the fear of not having familiar people around me in new situations.

The battle within is a great battle, but with a willing heart and mind, faith in God and strength and determination, this battle is a winnable one.

Bitterness can filter in through any open door of pain. But, no matter what you go through, guard your heart. In it flows the substance of life or death.

CHAPTER 9

THE DEPTH OF VISION

Someone once said to me, "Wherever you go, make sure they value your worth." That was a powerful statement that has remained etched in my mind. It is a constant reminder to me that when God ordains a direction for my life, there will always be someone there who values my worth.

Only a visionary will be able to see vision in your life. From whom are you receiving advice? Are there people surrounding you who value the worth that God has entrusted within you? Well, God does value your worth. That is why He created you with purpose that comes to fruition as you follow the vision designed for your life. Ask yourself, "Do I know the ordained vision for my life?" Are your actions and decisions moving you toward purpose, or are you randomly making choices?

Knowing and understanding the vision of promise and plan for your life will cause you to contend for the fruition of promise. When obstacles fight you, knowing the vision for your life will cause you to take a defensive posture of triumph. When challenges confront you and it seems like the opposite of what God has promised is manifesting, it will cause you to say, "But God, You are yet Lord of my life, and You are the *final* authority." It will cause the Word of God to rise up and for you to say, "The Word of God will not return void, but it will accomplish that which it sets out to do" on your behalf.

Knowing and understanding the depth of the vision for your life enables you to realize that God's purpose for your life goes far beyond you. It goes beyond feelings, although God does care about your feelings. But feelings cannot rule your thoughts, decisions, behavior, or beliefs. The vision for your life is not just for you, but for all those lives you are meant to touch and bring change to.

Vision is a deep sense of divine direction. Sadly, countless people feel that they do not know the direction for their lives. It is okay at a point in your life if you do not know, but do not give up without seeking to find your purpose. At one time I did not know what my purpose in life really was, but until I knew, I continued to walk in faith, truth, and the gifts granted by God.

It is imperative to know. When you do not know, your position is comparable to the saying that addresses one with no perspective: "Stand for something, or you will fall for anything." If you do not stand on vision (God's vision for your life) or are not aware of what it is, then it is easy to make random and reckless decisions. When you know and understand vision, and when you have the right perspective for life, you are more apt to guard it.

One way of knowing is to follow the steps of God: *"In all thy ways acknowledge Him, and He shall direct thy paths" (Proverbs 3:6).* Vision will keep you alive, both naturally and spiritually. When trouble and tests come, vision will make you stand and fight even when everything around you and inside of you says, "Give up!" Vision will cause you to trust God as your source. It will bring you to a place where when you find yourself right in the midst of intensive battles in life and battles against your mind saying that you cannot take it anymore, there is a push from within that will force you into a posture of winning at all costs and not accepting defeat as an alternative. Suddenly, just when it feels like your hands are slipping, there is a flashback of promise—the thoughts of where God has brought you from already—and the assurance of where He has promised to take you.

Then you find yourself in an offensive and defensive posture, warring to destroy the plans of the enemy against your life. You find yourself in heightened worship and praise. You discover that you do have strength left to war and walk in faith for what is rightfully yours. You find that you are willing to sit in the quiet peace and allow the glory of the Lord to envelop your whole being.

You find that because you are willing to fight and maintain your posture of faith, because of the vision, you are now willing to wait and hear the voice of God. You find that you are willing to wait on His direction. You are willing to not only hear, but also to obey. You understand that the vision for your life absolutely must come to pass. Your joy, strength, peace, and blessings are all connected to vision.

Not only that, but you also realize that the reason why the battle has intensified is that Satan knows you have intensified in greater strength! He knows that you are a threat to the kingdom of darkness because of your faith, knowledge of the Word, perseverance, and obedience to God. Perhaps you have not seen the manifestation of that greater power within yet, but get ready, because it is getting ready to manifest in extraordinary ways!

Satan sometimes realizes that you are a threat to his kingdom before *you* realize that you are a spiritual threat to his kingdom. The praying, fasting, giving, worshiping, and walking in obedience benefits more than just your present situations or battles. It benefits you entirely because it strengthens you in the power of Jesus Christ. It makes you more sensitive to the spirit realm as you live a consecrated life. It causes you to stand on the Word, wait, trust, and hear from God, rather than randomly rely on your own solutions. It even helps to raise your expectations of God's reliance. Now you are no longer wondering if He will show up. Instead, you expect Him to show up!

I remember over fifteen years ago when I received my first commission: "Evangelize and set My young people free." I remember that years later the Lord began to deal with me and commission me to women's ministry, particularly healing. During this time, there were several transitions underway in my family, especially with my having two small boys. But because of the mandates from God, I had a firm confirmation that God was with me and my family.

God gave me wisdom to walk in the call. I did not drop my boys off at different places, but for most of my ministry engagements, they were with me. It was a step-by-step process of faith, trust, and obedience that developed me. I could have used the boys as an excuse. Instead, I trusted that since God said it, He would provide the timing and the wisdom for me to do this. I did not drop my children off just anywhere and put ministry before them. But I waited on God and His timing.

Even in my willingness to obey the Lord, there were transitions and challenges that confronted me, even before the birth of my children. Any strategy can be used to keep you (and your seed) from your destined place. I remember the night before I had my oldest son; God woke me up about 2:00 a.m. I felt such a heart of worship and praise. I had no idea that I was going to have my son later that day. While I was up praying, the Spirit of the Lord just wrapped Himself around me. I even remember an intense travailing at some point and then back to worship and ministering to the Lord. And when I felt the release, I went back to bed.

Now during the time of carrying my son, I could hear the enemy say, "I'm going to kill you and your child." It was not an audible voice, but the voice or impression was just as strong as an audible one. I never told anyone this specifically during that time, but I stayed in the prayer lines and around those who were anointed. I stood on the Word of God and His promises to me and my seed.

During my delivery, suddenly the baby's monitor flatlined, and I no longer felt him moving. The pains had ceased for that moment. The doctors and nurses came running in; they made all kinds of calls and came from all directions of the hospital. But a short time later, everything was back to normal. I believe by waking up in obedience and through praying, worshiping, and standing on the promises of God because of the vision and plan God had for our lives, both my son and I were spared. The weapon formed, but it did not prosper.

Almost two years later, I had my second son. During the time that I carried him, I heard that same voice whisper in my ear and say, "I am going to kill you and your child." I knew that the terroristic threat of the enemy was rising again. I did not receive what he said.

One day, I had a telephone conversation with an anointed woman of God. She said that the Lord had told her to pray for me because the enemy wanted me and my child dead. I told her the same thing had happened with my first son. She prayed, and I felt a peace and comfort from the Lord.

On the day that my second son was born, before time for delivery, I was awakened again around 1:30 or 2:00 a.m. to worship and praise. Again I felt such an overwhelming call to prayer. After the worship and adoration, I remember my spirit began travailing. Again I had no knowledge that I was going to have my son later that day. After such a powerful prayer, I felt a release and went back to bed. Later in the morning, I quickly went into labor and had my second son. Both he and I were fine—so I thought.

After my stay in the hospital, both the boys and I went over to my mom's house so that she could help us acclimate. But while I was there, within a couple of days, my leg began to swell. My mom insisted that I not wait for the doctor's appointment a couple of days later, but to call him immediately. I did.

I called the doctor, described my condition, and he said, "Meet me at the hospital right away, and be prepared to be admitted." After I arrived at the hospital, they did tests, and my doctor told me that there was a blood clot that had broken off and was traveling from my leg; a piece had broken off and was traveling toward my heart and lungs. I was shocked hearing the news, but my reaction was yet one of peace. I began to remember being awakened to worship and the time of intercession. I was so grateful for being in a position to hear the Lord and trust Him and see the manifestation of God.

During my time of healing and recovery, a minister friend called me at my mom's house and began to minister to me regarding my second son. It was a powerful word of promise regarding his life and calling. And previously we had received ministry regarding our oldest son as well. Now I had another reason to contend for the vision. It was not just about me, but about my seeds. Isn't it amazing how threatened the enemy was? He never intended for any of us to see the vision of God unfold in our lives.

Because Satan knows the power of God, he seems to take it more seriously than we do. He will act against the Word that God has spoken over your life, even before you even fully understand the strength of the Word spoken by God over your life. He uses all the artillery he can to try to stop the vision from ever manifesting.

But you must understand the vision of God, the plan of God for your life and the life of your seed. You must understand that there is a daily battle waged against you, and in order to win, you must stay in the face of God. You will receive your instructions and strategies from Him. You must not add to or subtract from them, but you must follow them to the letter in order to see victory.

God taught me early on that I could not do what I wanted to do. He also taught me that my safety and blessings are in obedience to Him. I remember when I first got married. During the first year, I recall waiting for my husband to come home from choir rehearsal. I remember waiting and waiting. Back then we did not have cell phones, so I could not just call him. I remember feeling frustrated and anxious. I came from a large family, worked in almost every capacity at church, and was not used to just sitting and waiting. But I found that this was my weekly Saturday night routine.

One night, I said to myself, "Enough is enough." I remember it was about 9:00 to 9:30 p.m., and I grabbed my bag and keys and headed for the car. But to my surprise, when I went out the front door and turned the corner of the building on my way to my car, in one spot of the property I could feel hands on my chest pushing me back, and I heard in my spirit, "Go back; there's danger out there. Go back." I did not see a natural hand, but I felt those hands pushing me back. In my spirit, I heard that voice warning me, and I knew it was an angel of the Lord.

I turned around and went back upstairs. I sat on the bed and thought about what had just happened. I did not plan to go anywhere now. But I began to hear my flesh crying out: "You are tired of waiting around every Saturday night. Do you really want to be here when he gets home?" The more I listened, the angrier I got. I then picked up my jacket, grabbed my bag and keys, and headed out again.

I walked out the front door and turned the corner to head to my car, and in the exact same spot, I again felt those hands pushing me back. I again heard that voice in my spirit, saying the exact same thing: "Go back; there's danger out there. Go back." But this time, it was almost as if I closed my eyes and gritted my teeth, and I pushed past that spot. I chose to heed the anger of the flesh, rather than the warning of the Holy Spirit.

I got in my car and headed down the highway. I did not even have a destination. I just did not want to be home waiting. To me, it represented an act of desperation to continually sit and wait week after week (understand that I was young then, but this was a lesson that God ensured would be learned).

I continued driving for about an hour or so. It was now after midnight. I turned around and jumped back on the parkway going north. When I got on, it was almost as if someone took my face and turned it to my rearview mirror and said, "Take note of everything about this night. Take note of everything around you." It was as if I was viewing everything in slow motion for a while.

I remember seeing that there were a couple of cars on the highway in front of me and a couple in back of me. As I looked closer in the night, I could see a bus and a car behind me. Then I began to just feel strangeness in the night. I could feel eeriness in the air. It was a feeling that something was not right.

Again, I did take note of the cars around me and that bus. Suddenly there were no cars in front of me. So my headlights provided the only lights in front. I did see the bus and car approaching, but there was nothing unusual about that. Then suddenly out of nowhere, a car came out from the left side of the road! Where did it come from? It had not been on the highway before. And it flew out onto the middle of the parkway, with the driver erratically and repeatedly crossing all three lanes!

I knew what to do. I said to myself, "When he goes to the right, I will accelerate and pass him." But I just could not make it because of the speed and uncontrollable three-lane crossing the driver was doing. Then I looked up and noticed that the bus and other car had gotten past him. How did they make it past from behind me while I was still here with this crazy driver?

There were no other cars behind me. There was only darkness. Now it was just the two of us on the road. I did not know what to expect next. Then instantaneously he ended up on the right side of the road directly in front of me. His car flipped over right in front of me!

My immediate reaction was that someone could be hurt…or there could be some expectant mother in the car or a child. I had no choice but to stop, since the car had flipped over directly in front of me. I did not have to get out of the car though, but I did. Again, the concern for potential victims was in the forefront of my mind. My headlights stayed on as I stood outside my car near my door.

Then I yelled out, "Are you all right? Are you okay?" Then I heard the voice of the Lord say, "Get back in your car and lock your doors." That startled me! I jumped back into the car and locked my doors, and then a man crawled out the back of the flipped over car and slithered, like a snake, through the side of the grassy road. My mouth dropped open! I pulled off, reported the incident to the toll person, and needless to say, the entire hour's ride home, I repented and cried. I kept saying, "God, I'll never do it again." Tears were rolling down my face, knowing that the Lord had sent two warnings earlier that day. He had warned me about danger. I could have been killed in a car accident, or that man could have hurt or killed me when I stopped to see if anyone was hurt.

Was all of this worth my frantic behavior that caused me to leave home even though the Lord warned me not to? No! My thoughts were now that of gratitude and appreciation of God's mercy. That had been an out-and-out-defiance on my part because of my emotions! But because of grace and mercy, I lived to see many more years. I also had sense enough to know that it is a dangerous thing to take advantage of God's grace!

So on that day, I found out that my battles could not be fought in the natural, because my emotions would cause me to make wrong choices. God taught me through this situation that I should lift up to Him anything that presents itself as a problem in my life, rather than listen to the dictates of my flesh. Early on I learned that it is imperative to hear and obey the voice of God!

I find it so amazing how we can hear from God but still choose not to listen. We can feel that little check that says, "Don't do it." Yet, we still do. It is all because the flesh gets defensive when it feels hurt or discomfort. I heard the voice of the Lord warning me. And I felt the angels pushing me back, but because of the pride of flesh saying "I will not wait around again," I ended up facing danger and possibly death.

Many of you get upset with what you see or feel and decide to handle the situation yourself. Battles can be fought and won in the natural, but even so, some are temporary wins. Or they are wins only in certain areas of the battle, but not a complete victory. It is the power of God that holds the enemy back. Understanding your vision and fighting for it means self-sacrifice and most people are not willing to do that, which is why they will have sporadic victories in their lives rather than having and living victorious lives.

When my husband and I first married and moved into an apartment, the downstairs neighbors were unbelievable! As soon as we walked into the house, they would start banging on the ceiling and yelling, "Keep it down up there." My husband talked to them and let them know that we were in compliance with our lease concerning the floors' being carpeted. They did not care, and they kept harassing us. My husband spoke with them and with the super, who would talk with them, and they would stop the harassment for a while but start again.

Finally, one day I did some research on the legal aspects of harassment and found that it was time to take them to court. I had been praying about the situation and decided that this was the solution. We did go to court, and that couple acted like a vaudeville act. Neither the spectators nor the judge could believe what they were seeing and hearing. The judge just shook his head as they spoke.

Then after the judge reviewed the complaint concerning harassment, the defendant said, "Your Honor, I want a legal definition of harassment."

I immediately responded, "Your Honor, I have a legal definition from Black's Law Dictionary, which I did provide to the defendant when our complaint was filed."

The judge said to the defendant, "You are in trouble now! Are you sure you want to mess with them?" Of course, everyone had a good laugh with that. Then, the judge asked me if I wanted to fine them. My response was, "Your Honor, I just want them to stop harassing us."

In all of this, sometimes it was a challenge to keep the flesh under subjection. But the Holy Spirit allowed us to yet exemplify the principles of Christ throughout this entire ordeal. This is not to say that it would have been wrong for them to be fined, but in following the leading of God, I was able to glean a deeper revelation from everything that happened.

For a few months afterwards, there was peace—no harassment. Then months later, we had dinner guests over, and those neighbors started banging on the ceiling. This time I really did not feel peace, but anger. Although the guests were family and close friends, it was still a frustrating situation to deal with (don't walk . . . don't have other people over . . .)—and this while still trying to portray Christianity.

So the next day I caught this woman in the hall, and yes, I did wait to hear her going for the mail. I approached her, and I was very angry. I addressed her about both her and her husband's behavior and told her that we would see her in court again. The more I talked, the more the Holy Spirit tugged at me to let it go and go back upstairs. Thankfully, I eventually did listen.

When we had the second appearance in court, we received the same favor from the judge. He reprimanded the defendants and ruled on our behalf again. But when I got home, the Lord began to speak to me, saying, "Do you want to go through this again?"

I said, "No, God, I do not want to keep going through this. I want this to end today." God said, "The natural resources are fine (court) sometimes, but you have got to realize that this battle is not in the natural, but in the Spirit."

The Lord began to let me know that I was using a natural solution to win a spiritual battle. Even as we utilize natural resources, we should still exercise our authority in the Spirit over all that affects our lives. Satan loves to steal our peace and joy and will use anyone available. Yes, the court systems exist for order and justice, but sometimes the verdicts may not be just. Thankfully, the judge ruled in our favor both times, and I believe we even fined them the second time. However, it was not until I sealed this victory in prayer and praise that we won!

Immediately after the Lord spoke this to me, I dropped to my knees and declared there would be peace as long as we lived there. I declared that we would never have to go to court again for this situation, in the name of Jesus. I took authority over the enemy and from that day until we moved, there was peace. Sadly, both the defendants ended up sick, and one was carried out and died, we were told. The other ended up in a nursing home, we were told. But the Bible says, *"Touch not mine anointed..."* (Psalm 105:15) and when you are given a chance to get it right but you do not, the consequences of sin do prevail in your life. My regret is that it could have been different. We could have been the ones to go to the grocery store for them or to be a blessing to them in other ways. But despite our efforts, they would see us, say "God bless you," then continue to harass us. Yet God was the final authority for us.

When you understand God's vision for your life, you will have to understand that the battles that come do not always have easy natural solutions. You think it is the marriage, but the enemy is really after the vision. You think it is finances, but the enemy is after the vision. You think it is your children, but the enemy is after the vision for your life and the generations here and to come. The battle goes deeper than fighting in the natural. It goes deeper than you. Remember, your choices can affect your seeds and others that you can reach.

"Put on the whole armor of God, that ye may be able to stand against the wiles of the devil. For we wrestle not against flesh and blood, but against principalities, against powers, against the rulers of the darkness of this world, against spiritual wickedness in high places. Wherefore take unto you the whole armor of God, that ye may be able to withstand in the evil day, and having done all, to stand" (Eph. 6:11–13). Understand that if you were not so powerful and victorious, Satan would not fight you so hard. Your victory is not predicated upon what you see, but it is predicated upon what God has said about you.

If you want to know what He has said, read the Word of God. Deuteronomy 28 lets you know that you are blessed in your coming and going. It lets you know that you are the head and not the tail. It lets you know that God will make provisions for you and for your family. There is an abundance of promises all throughout the Bible. But there are those who will not read it. And still others will not study to get an understanding. Then there are others who refuse to believe it. The Word of God is so powerful that its wisdom is noted throughout various quotes in society today, and many quoting do not even realize that what they are saying is from the Word!

Jesus is so powerful! Have you ever noticed that profane language is used with the name *Jesus* or reference *God* or *holy*? These are aspects of the Word, which Satan hates. So he has individuals use these names and words attributed to God's attributes in profane ways and disrespect. Have you ever noticed that the names of other religious gods are never taken in vain like this? Satan has spent centuries trying to destroy the essence of love and power through God Jehovah and His Son, Jesus Christ. The Word of God is powerful! The name of Jesus is powerful! Satan hates it and will do anything he can to lessen its power and influence.

Even for your life, if Satan did not know that there was greatness beyond your failures, joy beyond your pain and triumph beyond your tears, he would not fight you so hard with trouble! The problem is that most people allow their natural situations, problems, trials, and tests to dictate who they are as sons and daughters of God.

Holding on to the divine vision of God for your life guarantees success in your life—not success according to man's standards, but God's. Man measures success only by career, money, family, and material possessions; but while being abundant in those areas, he still lacks integrity, compassion, peace, health, wholeness, and morality, to name a few things. Abundant life in Christ will exemplify the attributes of God, fruit of the Spirit, blessings, and favor. In other words, wholeness in your mind and emotions, healing and empowerment, peace, joy, a renewed mind, and a transformed life, as well as having your heart's desires, are some of the benefits of the kingdom for you as you hold fast to vision!

CHAPTER 10

EMPOWERED TO CHANGE

Inside all of us is the natural God-given ability and priceless gift of choice. Even a baby does not have to be taught to choose. In various options, he naturally acknowledges his preferences. Even more natural and amazing is that child's ability to learn and properly use the word "*no.*" He may have heard the parent or guardian use that word. However, I find it amazing that this baby, at only a few months old, can express his answer "no" by moving his head in the opposite direction of the spoon when it has something on it that he does not like or want. I find it fascinating that before he can express "no," he can demonstrate it by tossing a toy away or pushing away a bottle of water over juice or milk. Sometimes he may move his upper torso to the side of the high chair and then to the other side, away from the object or food, in order to express "no." Then as he grows a little older and begins to form his words, it seems ever so easy for him to actually verbalize "no." Yet no one took this child and rehearsed his behavior or speech as repeated conditioning. This child's natural instinct seems to understand that he has a choice.

I find it even more amazing that toddlers are constantly taking advantage of the freedom and power of choice, whether it is for their benefit or not. They will express what they want or like and what they do not want or like, ever so freely. If you are in the mall and they are tired, their behavior will soon demonstrate that they are tired. I have seen some children literally fall prostrate on the floor in protest of something that they wanted or did not want to do. This is yet again another demonstration of a child's liberated use of choice. Yet as adolescents and adults, it seems like the liberation of choice is forgotten because of peer pressure, personal issues, fear, or the desire to be accepted.

When you maintain and utilize the natural ability of choice, you have the power to change your life. Yes, there are situations that fight you when it comes time to change, but if you understand that positive change will benefit your life, you will be more apt to fight in order to bring about the change. Although fear can initiate change, not everyone is moved to change because of fear. It still takes the actual action of choice in order to bring about change. There has to be a conscious effort to change.

In the case where a woman is abused, she may have experienced a cycle of repeated negative results, such as unsuccessful attempts of getting away. Or she may fear the consequences and backlash from her abuser if she is caught. Therefore, feeling useless and helpless in the situation, she soon accepts the situation. Although she may feel trapped, she gives up on her right to bring change into her life when she feels like her situation cannot change because of what she has experienced in the past.

Giving up because of consistent negative responses or negative outcomes can consequently result in submissive behavior from the victim. Through conditioning caused by negative responses, the victim has learned to submit to abuse. She has learned to embrace a false reality that her life cannot change, although shelters, help lines, organizations, and churches are available for assistance.

An imprisoned mind does not exercise its God-given ability of choice. An imprisoned heart does not even believe that it has the right or privilege of choice. Therefore, degradation or fear may not cause individuals to react as many think they should. Instead, exercising the power of choice brings about the desired response for change.

Oftentimes it seems like negative choices are so easy to make. It seems as if at any given time, you can easily choose to do something contrary to God's purpose and will for your life. At these times, it is easy to choose; it is easy to feel or see a quick manifestation. These choices may produce temporary worldly pleasures, according to the Bible. Understand that the Word does acknowledge that wrong choices can offer pleasures, although on a temporary basis and sometimes destructive basis. However, it seems as if when faced with a choice to change in order to benefit your life and even those around you, your mind, your will, your flesh, and your environment fight those choices. Let's look at what Paul said in the Bible:

For I know that nothing good dwells within me, that is, in my flesh. I can will what is right, but I cannot perform it. [I have the intention and urge to do what is right, but no power to carry it out.] For I fail to practice the good deeds I desire to do, but the evil deeds that I do not desire to do are what I am [ever] doing. Now if I do what I do not desire to do, it is no longer I doing it [it is not myself that acts], but the sin [principle] which dwells within me [fixed and operating in my soul]. So I find it to be a law (rule of action of my being) that when I want to do what is right and good, evil is ever present with me and I am subject to its insistent demands.

—Romans 7:18–21 AMP

What this is saying is that when you want to make the right choice, sin or evil is there to buffet you to try to cause you to make the wrong choice. This is saying that even Paul, one of the greatest Biblical leaders of all time, also had choices to make. Regardless of our titles or stature, we are all confronted with making the right choices.

I often caution my sons not to fall for the cliché "We all make mistakes" but to understand this cliché to its fullest entitlement. Yes, we are all human and will make mistakes. However, not all negative actions are mistakes. Some are just blatant choices—wrong choices. And choices (seeds), whether good or bad, produce consequences (fruit). Your choice or action is an actual seed that *you* have planted for your life. Also, erroneous decisions can be made because of another's enticing deception. However, sometimes you may be informed, have all the details concerning the consequences, and still move forward with the wrong choice. Be careful! Choice is very powerful! And, some "mistakes," or choices, are more costly than others. Are you willing to pay that price?

Choice can decide if you are going to end up in abundance or lack. Choice can decide whether you end up with a prestigious career or a meaningless job. Choice can decide if you will end up in a loving relationship or abusive one. Choice can determine whether you are a religious churchgoer or a son or daughter with a meaningful relationship with God. Choice can determine if your life is empowered or imprisoned. Choice is powerful!

The problem with some of those living in ashes is that multitudes have tried to change by themselves. They have based all their actions on their own strength rather than the strength of Jesus Christ. He is the source of power and strength.

Many of you have been fighting in your own strength based on the reasoning of your mind or following the dictates of your emotions. However, when you accept Jesus Christ into your life to lead you and guide you, you are empowered through God's strength to make the best decisions. It is His strength that enables you to change and even gives you the courage and strength to change for a greater quality of life. He will provide you with strategy.

Empowerment is to be granted authority and ability. It is sanctioning. You are sanctioned by God to walk in the power and authority of Jesus Christ and have abundance, or wholeness, in your life. Through the Holy Spirit, who was the power that carried out the creation as God spoke and willed in Genesis, you can invoke change in your life.

As a believer, you must understand that it is not you who destroys the yoke. It is the anointing (of God within you) that destroys the yoke: *"And it shall come to pass in that day, that his burden shall be taken away from off thy shoulder, and his yoke from off thy neck, and the yoke shall be destroyed because of the anointing"* (Isa. 10:27). A yoke is that which controls and binds you. Through Jesus Christ, you now have *exousia* (Greek, power), which is authority, right, or privilege, through the Word of God. You also have *dunamis* (Greek, power), which is might, action, or force, through the Holy Spirit that actually carries out the manifestation of the Word of God (Luke 10:19).

As we discussed in previous chapters, when you abide in God and His Word abides in you, you can ask what you want according to the Word of God, and you shall have it. The Holy Spirit recognizes your words when your life is aligned with God and your request is according to the will (Word) of God. You are under the banner, which is the blood of Jesus, through the cross.

Corporations have logos, flags, or banners that cause them to be identified. That banner defines who they are and all that is associated with them. When you accept Jesus Christ, your life comes under the banner of Jesus. The cross and the blood of Jesus, signifies who you are and with whom you are associated, and it causes people to recognize all that is associated with your new life. The Holy Spirit recognizes that banner, and so does Satan. The Word of God says, *"When the enemy shall come in like a flood, the Spirit of the Lord shall lift up a standard [banner] against him"* Isaiah 59:19. God will cause the enemy to remember that you are one of His and that he no longer has any rights to your life. The weapon may form against you, but it shall not prosper. This means that unless it is a situation that God allows and that He will turn around for your good, Satan is then trespassing, and you have the right to kick him out! This means he has to go, as well as let go of any situation that he tries to bring against you and hold you hostage to. As a believer, you now have power. This is the actual demonstration or manifestation of the authority of the Word in your life.

Sadly, some believers never reach this place. They lie down in their situation and wave the white flag of defeat. They confess but never possess their inheritance or apply the power in their own situations. Possession is ownership. You can be willed a beautiful home. Your name is on the deed. But if you never take possession or claim of the property, you never experience the joy of ownership. God has willed a great inheritance to you through the death, burial, and resurrection of Jesus Christ. Through Jesus, *you* are now::

1. Joint heirs (Rom. 8:17). This means that you are a son or daughter of God. This means that the same spiritual authority that Jesus operates in, you can operate in, with God as your father.
2. Endowed with power by receiving the gift of the Holy Spirit (Acts 2:1-4; Luke 24:49; 10:19).
3. Victorious when you follow the principles of God. If you keep the Word of God, you will have good success (Josh. 1:8).
4. More than a conqueror (Rom. 8:37). All things are working together for your good when you love the Lord and live according to His purpose (Rom. 8:28). All things that come your way that are not in accordance to the will of God will be turned around for your benefit rather than lead to your demise.
5. A recipient of eternal life (John 3:16).
6. A candidate for abundant life (John 10:10).
7. Surrounded in love and protection (Isaiah 59:19)

Understanding who you are and whose you are will change your life. Renewing your mind through the Word of God helps your understand who you are. Learning about the relationship that God wants you to have with Him helps you understand whose you are and how much God loves you.

Empowerment means that you have the ability to refrain from lying down to die, but you stand and fight! You understand that you are not just haphazardly here, but that you were created for purpose and created with purpose. Therefore, you recognize the satanic tactics, strategies, and devices that he uses to distract you and prevent you from change.

Now you can understand that cycles can be broken in your life. It is a matter of choice! It was never God's purpose for your life to go in endless and useless destructive cycles. It was never God's will for you to live under bondage and oppression. I find that those who hear this type of message and still render excuses why they cannot change are simply under the vices and the grip of an ensnared mind.

There are those who find it easier to make excuses and stay in bondage than to fight and move forth in change as directed by God. Bondage can be abuse, oppression, depression, addictions, low self-esteem, fear, or anything else that prohibits you from excelling. God intended for you to be free! *"Thou wilt keep him in perfect peace, whose mind is stayed on thee: because he trusteth in thee"* (Isa. 26:3). The Word of God has an answer for everything you could possibly face.

I find it very interesting to examine some psychological systems used by scientists and professors. For example, in the area of phobias, the process of systematic desensitization has been explored. Its goal is to reduce phobic anxiety responses to that which a person fears. This process weakens the association between the stimulus and the conditioned response to fear. This helps the patients or clients deal with their phobias by renewing their minds to lessen their reactions to the fear or stimulus. This is done by systematic hierarchy and imagery, as well as relaxation. Over a number of sessions, patients are conditioned to move from fear to relaxation when they are confronted with their phobias.

I say all of that to say that your mind is powerful! By simply confronting the fear through conditioning and causing you to view it in a different perspective, the fear is reduced. Scientists and psychologists are constantly studying in order to find lasting solutions for emotional or behavioral issues people face. Your mind is more powerful than you realize.

Reevaluating and reconditioning the way you think, perceive, and react, basing it on biblical principles, can awaken you to so many positive elements of life! And this will benefit your entire life and the lives of those you are meant to impact. Your gift of choice is powerful: *"If the Son therefore shall make you free, ye shall be free indeed"* (John 8:36). Through what Jesus did on the cross, you are entitled to freedom and all the benefits of the kingdom of God when you are a son or daughter of God.

Thus the question remains "Why are so many yet living in bondage? The answer is because they choose to. You are not the only one going through your situation. There are others who have gone through what you are going through, and they survived. They have lived to tell their story of victory. Their will was to live and not just to survive!

Others are in bondage because of a lack of understanding and knowledge, because of misinformation. Hosea 4:6 reads, "*My people are destroyed for lack of knowledge.*" But today you no longer have that excuse! So no longer live with that bondage that God never intended, regardless of how you got there. Your life, your bloodline, and your seed (children and generations to come) can be delivered from this prison.

This takes honesty. It is not always easy to be honest—with yourself, most of all. You may be wonderful in convincing everyone else that it is all right. But when your head hits that pillow at night, you, God, and Satan know the real truth. Stop living a façade, and access your right to your inheritance—divine love, peace, provision, and wholeness—through Jesus Christ.

So choose today to make positive changes. Surrender your mind to God. Through Jesus Christ, you have the power to command your mind and body to come into subjection to the will of Jesus Christ for your life. I always make this confession: "I have the mind of Christ" (Phil. 2:5). Know that every situation that you are going through and even any situation that could confront you in the future have already been resolved in the Word of God. Every answer has been given and every way made through Jesus when He defeated Satan on the cross. Rise up and walk in the empowerment that God has given you. It is time for a change! If you do this, out of your ashes, you *will rise!*

CHAPTER 11

ESCAPING AND DESTROYING GENERATIONAL CURSES

＿＿＞

Generational curses were briefly mentioned in prior chapters. However, I wanted to dedicate an entire chapter to this subject. I believe that this is necessary in order for you to fully comprehend the plan of Satan to capture or recapture your life through the bondages of those issues that are in your bloodline.

All of us have generational curses throughout our bloodline. It could be an addiction such as drugs or alcohol. It can be pride or rebellious natures, the Internet, gambling, or sex. It could also be issues such as curses of poverty or lack, or histories of divorces throughout your family line. Have you ever seen a family, or perhaps it may even be yours, where the women were always falling for abusive men? Let us say that you have seen your grandmother, aunts, or mother establish relationships with abusive men. Then you begin to examine your own relationships, and suddenly what *you* are now living becomes all too familiar. That is because you recognize that you have now accepted the same destructive patterns that other women in your family have. A pattern of negative, destructive behavior or issues that continually plague a bloodline and is the primary avenue of destruction in that bloodline is a generational curse.

Another issue that can be seen through various bloodlines is negligence. There are men (and also women) who choose to live under the curse of their fathers, grandfathers, great-grandfathers, uncles, or cousins by choosing to avoid responsibility. Some men may stay with their families, yet they are absentee fathers and husbands. They will not establish relationships with their wives or children. They never support the children at school or in extracurricular activities. They never show appreciation to their wives. Their hearts are not connected to what has been given to them.

Still other men choose to leave, as they accept the generational curse plotted against their lives. The Bible says that a *"A double-minded man is unstable in all of his ways"* (James 1:8, emphasis added). Until his mind comes into subjection to the place that God designed for man, he will always live under that generational curse that tells him to take the easy way out and leave. His mind will always justify his actions.

Sometimes people get confused as to whether they are living under a generational curse. If they do not find themselves taking the *same exact* actions as their fathers, mothers, grandfathers, grandmothers, uncles, aunts, or cousins, then they cannot accept the fact that they are living under a curse. For instance, if a grandfather is an alcoholic, his son has a choice of adopting that behavior or escaping from the behavior. He saw his father come home drunk all the time. He saw that this behavior caused his dad to be irresponsible in the home. He saw his mother unhappy because she had to pull the weight of the family. So this son makes up his mind that he will never drink as his father did. But as life goes on, this son finds himself operating in excessive behavior through lust and women.

Instead of this son facing his problems, he buries them through his relationships with various women. His behavior becomes obsessive. His database is full of women that he can call, meet or e-mail. He never has a steady relationship. He does not respect women but uses them for sex. One day he decides that he should settle down and marry, since his friends all have. He even begins to believe that marriage will change his actions. However, his faithfulness lasts only a little while because of his obsessive behavior with women. A natural desire has become perverted.

This represents undisciplined behavior and obsession (lust). He carried this baggage and behavior into his marriage. At first he looked for anything to pacify those feelings: his wife's Victoria's Secret magazine, TV ads, wrestling (to see the women), and other magazines. Then he turned to the Internet and pornography. He established outside relationships with only women. Finally, he actually cheated on his wife, and the compulsion continued.

In the meantime, his son is watching all of this. His son sees that his dad is not interested in his school activities or sports. His dad is not interested in their family outings. He sees that something does have his dad preoccupied but knows that it does not involve him. He sees that their house is really not a home; although dad is there, he is absent from the family. This son knows his own hurt and also sees the pain of his mother.

This third-generation grandson vows that he will not end up like his grandfather or father. He declares that he will be a family man. He makes up his mind that he will be disciplined and balanced and will stay away from alcohol or anything else destructive or addictive. He does not want his future wife and children to experience the heartache that he has experienced.

Now this third-generation grandson grows up, goes to college, gets married, and establishes a family. He is there for his family. He wants to provide anything and everything that he can for his wife and children in order for them to be happy. Therefore, he constantly drives himself to success.

He is always bettering himself in school. He is always forging ahead at work. He is now a pivotal player in his corporation, as he continually rises with more and more responsibilities. There is nothing that he would not do for his company and family, and he is being well rewarded. With all the drive that he has, he continues to improve and grow. There is nothing more that he could ask for. He feels that his world is far better than the one he grew up in.

One day he looks at his home, cars, boat, and SUV. He thinks about his children in the best schools, and he thinks about all the wonderful vacations and experiences that he has provided for his family. He takes pride in knowing that his wife can buy anything she wants. He reviews his career, and nothing could be better.

But one day as he is thinking, his young son (fourth-generation great-grandson) interrupts his thoughts when he walks slowly into the room. He pauses and looks up at his dad and says, "So, you're home today, Dad? You mean, you don't have to work today?"

Then he moves closer to his dad, looks up, and says, "Dad, I know that you are working to make us happy. But rather than buying me that new bike, I would rather see you at my game. And are you going to be at Thanksgiving this year? Dad, I love you, but last Thanksgiving you missed most of the fun because you had to be out of town on business and got back late. Dad, we don't see you like we used to. And Mom is always crying. She said that this is not what she thought it would be like."

Then Dad takes a deep breath and stops everything as he sits down next to his son. He ponders for a moment and then suddenly sees himself as a boy in the face of his son. He now understands that the same obsessive, addictive behavior that he saw in his grandfather with the alcohol and in his father, who lived under the entanglement of lust, with women and sex, has now begun to infiltrate his life through obsessive, addictive work habits.

He was so determined that he would not be like them, but he became so obsessive in building a career and comfortable life that he forgot to maintain a healthy balance in life. Through this obsessive behavior, he constantly worked long hours in order to always travel, excel, and give his family everything that he did not have. He then realizes that he has accepted this generational curse.

The obsessive, addictive behavior began with alcohol, continued with sex, and now has ties with obsessive work habits. There is nothing wrong with working hard and making sacrifices, but you must have a balanced life. This behavior began to tear apart his family, just as in generations before. His wife was not happy, just like his mom and grandmother had not been happy as they watched these obsessions sever their family, as they watched their men submit to another generation of addiction.

But the difference is that when this third-generation grandson became aware of the strategy of destructive behavior in his bloodline, he began to gain leverage as he put balance back into his life. As he put priorities in order, he began to see his family coming together. He began to see not just happiness, but joy, in the faces of his wife and son.

The difference is that this man decided to escape the clutches of this generational curse. He understood that it was a matter of choice! Now this will be an example to his son (fourth-generation great-grandson) that when a problem arises, the power of choice is always available. In this man's case, he learned that if he would balance and prioritize things in his life, he could be successful, be available to his family, and live free from generational curses in their bloodline. And because of his willingness to accept the fact that he had been living under this curse, he was able to face the road to recovery.

A young woman may be frustrated with herself because her relationships always seem to go in the same cycle. She may wonder why it is that she is attracted to men who use her and then leave her and never commit to her. Although she may not want to always yield to those men who do not have good intentions, she may find that she does. Then as she looks into her bloodline, she sees how her relatives have always enticed the opposite sex, with seducing spirits. She, too, is one who loves to seduce. Although she appears to be a lady on the outside, the way that she walks, talks, and dresses reveals that she has an underlying seducing spirit that she often yields to.

Then this young woman looks at her mother, who always felt that she had to sleep with men in order to gain. Although her mother had a good job, she still felt the need to just be appreciated. So she would meet these men from various circles and end up in stale relationships with them. This daughter saw the men bringing pretty little boxes to her mother's house and eventually ending up in her mother's bedroom. She saw how "happy" her mother was when she received the attention from these men. Then, without fail, within a couple of months, the relationship was over. This left her mother heartbroken, always thinking that this man was "the one." This was a continuous cycle. But her mother never ended up with "the one."

Now this young woman's desire to feel loved has opened the door to her own quest. Since she never experienced the love of her father, she searches for love in any man's arms. It could also be a woman who simply does not have confidence in herself. Anyway, this daughter is also a hard worker, like her mom was. But after work, she is a lost soul struggling to find peace with being unconditionally loved.

This young woman submits to those men who say those special words, "I love you." If they show interest and bring flowers or perhaps sometimes take her out, she submits to their desires without thought. The need to be loved far outweighs any common sense.

Now she finds that she has three children by various men. Her life is completely different from what she had planned. But even after looking at herself and her children, she cannot seem to break the pattern that has plagued the women in her family for years. The feeling of self-worth and value did not come from their own growth and accomplishments. It did not even come from the value and purpose that God ordained. However, the estimated value was based strictly on whether there was a man in their lives to make them feel special. The true danger is not in appreciating a compliment from the opposite sex. But the true danger is not knowing that if on this day you do not receive a compliment, support, or encouragement from the opposite sex, that you are still special and important because God created you that way.

Let us look at King David. One day he saw Bathsheba bathing on the rooftop, and lust filled his heart. His desire for her caused him to plot against her husband. He began a relationship with Bathsheba while her husband was in battle. Then later when he found out that she was pregnant, he tried to force her husband, Uriah, to go home in hopes that he would go and make love to his wife. But Uriah felt obligated to the battle and stayed in the fight. Then David plotted Uriah's death and forced Uriah to go to the frontline of battle and Uriah was killed. David embraced the spirit of lust. Then lust gained entrance and escorted in deceit and murder.

God showed Nathan in a vision what David had done. Prophet Nathan was sent to David by God with the instructions to tell David all that he saw:

> *And the Lord sent Nathan to David. He came and said to him, There were two men in a city, one rich and the other poor. The rich man had very many flocks and herds, but the poor man had nothing but one little ewe lamb which he had bought and brought up, and it grew up with him and his chil-*

dren. It ate of his own morsel, drank from his own cup, lay in his bosom, and was like a daughter to him.

Now a traveler came to the rich man, and to avoid taking one of his own flock or herd to prepare for the wayfaring man who had come to him, he took the poor man's lamb and prepared it for his guest.

Then David's anger was greatly kindled against the man, and he said to Nathan, As the Lord lives, the man who has done this is a son [worthy] of death. He shall restore the lamb fourfold, because he did this thing and had no pity.

Then Nathan said to David, You are the man! Thus says the Lord, the God of Israel: I anointed you king of Israel, and I delivered you out of the hand of Saul. And I gave you your master's house, and your master's wives into your bosom, and gave you the house of Israel and of Judah; and if that had been too little, I would have added that much again. Why have you despised the commandment of the Lord, doing evil in His sight? You have slain Uriah the Hittite with the sword and have taken his wife to be your wife. You have murdered him with the sword of the Ammonites. Now, therefore, the sword shall never depart from your house, because [you have not only despised My command, but] you have despised Me and have taken the wife of Uriah the Hittite to be your wife.

Thus says the Lord, Behold, I will raise up evil against you out of your own house; and I will take your wives before your eyes and give them to your neighbor, and he shall lie with your wives in the sight of this sun. For you did it secretly, but I will do this thing before all Israel and before the sun. [Author's note: fulfilled in 2 Sam. 16:21–22]

And David said to Nathan, I have sinned against the Lord.

And Nathan said to David, The Lord also has put away your sin; you shall not die. Nevertheless, because by this

*deed you have utterly scorned the Lord and given great
occasion to the enemies of the Lord to blaspheme, the child
that is born to you shall surely die.*

—2 Samuel 12:1–14 AMP

The rich man represented David, and the poor man represented
Uriah. The rich man took from the poor man's flock rather than give
the weary traveler from his own. In listening to this story Nathan
told, David thought that the rich man should be put to death. He
thought that it was a terribly selfish act against the poor man, who
was simply trying to live. After hearing David's responsive dismay,
Nathan turned to him and said, "That man is you."

So David's deceit had covered his eyes as well. He had lived
in denial. He chose not to see the horror of his actions until Nathan
painted a clear picture. Again, you must understand that deception
deceives the offender first! Satan wants you to continue in sin and
error. He wants you to live in lack. He wants you to live in failure
and bondage. He wants to keep you blind to his destructive vices.
But when you allow him to use you, he has already deceived you.

Although David repented, there was a consequence to his household. He planted a destructive seed in his bloodline. He opened the
door to generational curses for his children. Even his firstborn son
with Bathsheba died because of his actions. And there were other
events in his family that shows that the curse continued throughout
his bloodline.

Next, his son Amnon lusted after his sister Tamar. The Bible
said that he "loved" Tamar. Certainly, this was not the unconditional
love of God. This was lust. True love is a giving, sacrificial love. It
does not pervert or abuse. It is devotion. But Amnon's lust burned so
greatly that he became mentally and emotionally ill with his burning
toward his sister.

Then his so-called friend reminded him that he was the king's
son with position and power. So they devised a plot to lure Tamar
into Amnon's room by bringing him food, as he pretended to be
physically sick. When she did come to his room to bring him the

food, he dismissed all the servants and guards, and he raped his sister. She pleaded with him not to do this. But he did.

Then after he did, he threw her out of his room and told his servants to bolt the door behind her. After the act, he now despised her. Tamar said that throwing her out afterward hurt more than the act itself. He stole her dignity and self-respect. She felt degraded. She did not feel worthy any longer of wearing her garments, which denoted royalty and purity.

So David's son embraced that spirit of thievery, deception, and lust, which had been welcomed by David. But Satan still had more plans for him and his family. This lust was coupled with perversion. Amnon's heart was hardened against his sister after the act, and he then despised her. Now hatred also filtered its way into the bloodline.

This perversion stripped David's daughter Tamar of any self-worth. Her virtue was stolen. She felt that she had nothing else of value left in her life, and the Bible says that she went to her room and there remained. This act destroyed her. She never recovered.

Despite the attempt to understand her pain, I still find it amazing that she was in the palace, was the king's daughter of royal blood, had servants at her disposal and had countless wealth and honor and everything else that the kingdom held at her reach, yet in her room is where she remained. If you are honest, there may have been situations that you experienced where you no longer wanted to face the world either. Your loss, hurt, betrayal—your ashes—may have left you weary, isolated and hopeless. But if you reach forward, you can pull yourself up with the strength of God!

Tamar never accepted the strength to reach out and move forward. She made the choice to die. She died emotionally and psychologically before her physical death. Many people are the same way. They have such a great inheritance through the covenant of God, yet they never embrace it because of the pain that they feel.

Many of you have forgotten who you are—a son or daughter of purpose. Many of you do not utilize the power and authority granted through salvation and the Holy Spirit. I understand that Tamar was filled with shame and did not want the discussion of this horrendous act to get out. She, no doubt, did not even want to face the reality of what had happened. However, she did not have to stay there in that condition. She could have come out of her ashes. As you can see, the enemy continued to filter through the bloodline of David, all because he opened the door.

Next, you have Absalom, who heard about his sister's rape and killed his brother Amnon. Prophet Nathan had warned that there would be blood in David's house. Just as David severed Uriah's family, now his family was being severed. David had repented. David was still anointed. However, he did sow seeds that sprang up in his bloodline. Again, the spiritual principles of God do not change for anyone. You will reap the harvest of the seeds that you sow.

Furthermore, even David's other son, Solomon, one of the wisest men who ever lived, embraced this curse. He had seven hundred wives and three hundred concubines. The Lord warned him not to mix with the women who did not believe in the true and living God, but Solomon did not listen. Instead, he heeded his own lusts:

But King Solomon [defiantly] loved many foreign women— the daughter of Pharaoh, women of the Moabites, Ammonites, Edomites, Sidonians, and Hittites.

—1 Kings 11:1 AMP

Did not Solomon king of Israel act treacherously against God and miss the mark on account of such women? Among many nations there was no king like him. He was loved by his God, and God made him king over all Israel; yet strange women even caused him to sin [when he was old he turned treacherously away from the Lord to other gods, and God rent his kingdom from him].

—Nehemiah 13:26 AMP

For this act, the kingdom of Israel was divided, as was prophesied. Generational curses are powerful if you receive them. They will continue to flow in your family until your family is destroyed.

It is Satan's job to devalue anyone and everyone that he can. But you must understand that you do not have to live under a generational curse. In Exodus 34:7, the Bible says that the sins of the fathers will be visited upon their children to the third and fourth generations. That means that the children will also experience the repercussions of their fathers' sins. Judgment is pronounced.

Then later, in Deuteronomy 24:16, the Bible says, *"The fathers shall **not** be put to death for the children, neither shall the children be put to death for the fathers: **every man** shall be put to death for **his own sin"** (emphasis added; also read Ezek. 18:20). Instead, each person will be *accountable for his own actions* and will reap the consequences accordingly. Therefore, you are no longer enslaved in the negative or destructive behavior of past generations. You have a choice!

For those people who yet look at generational curses as an excuse for their behavior, as an excuse not to change, God has already raised up many more who can testify that you do have a choice. Again, the mind is a powerful tool or weapon. What you receive is how you feed. What you digest is what your life will manifest. So it is important to renew your mind in positive teachings based on the principles of the Word of God.

The first step to healing is to admit that you are living under a generational curse. It is important to recognize that there is an issue in your bloodline that has penetrated your life by your acceptance. Next, it is imperative to forgive those in your bloodline who have accepted this curse and caused it to become familiar behavior to you. Forgiveness frees you from continually looking back and reliving the bondage. Forgiveness frees your mind from the past in order to liberate it for the present and future. Therefore, you must forgive them and recognize that it was their choice, but now you can make your own. Praise God!

Just like there are generational curses, there are also generational blessings that can be unleashed through prayer, acceptance of purpose, God's Word, and the renewing of your mind. When your children and family look at you, how do they perceive you? Do they see that you are lazy and never try to help yourself? Or do they see that you are one with great potential but who always uses excuses and never excels? When you speak, do your family and friends stop and take note? Or do they feel that you are all talk and no action? Would your family and friends say that you are a leader or a follower? Would they say that you live for now or that you live for now as you plan for the future? Basically, what I am trying to say is that *you*, by example, can be the one to break any negative cycle in your family bloodline.

I believe the freeing and liberating Word of God helps you understand your God-given right not to live under any generational curses. Once you understand who you are in God and that He has an ordained purpose for you, then you will realize that His plan does not include the baggage of generational curses. Then you can understand that you are not called to failure, but to success. You are not called to sorrow, but to joy. Again, this is not to say that this world will not present its share of hurt and disappointment. But it means that hurts and disappointments are not your final destined place. A calling is what your life has been purposed for. A calling is that special assignment that God has purposed for your hands and your life, which will give God the glory as you inherit the benefits.

Many people find it so hard to stand on the Word of God and principles of God because society has taught that being a Christian is a life of bondage. They feel that because you are encouraged as a Christian not to delve into certain behaviors of the flesh, then you are brainwashed and enslaved. But I find it interesting to know that now society is attempting to deal with the same ills that the Bible warned about and provided solutions for thousands of years ago.

The term *Christian* denotes Christ-like behavior and thought through the demonstration of His love and life. Therefore, walking in spiritual principles of the Word is as liberating as you can get here on this earth! The purpose of God's principles is to prevent you from going through unnecessary pain and struggle, which was never intended for your life. How many times have wrongful decisions been made that opened the door to great pain in your life?

Again, blessings can also follow down a bloodline, just like curses. My dad's life was an illustration of that. When I was a little girl, my dad had an accident on his job at Port Newark, New Jersey. He was working on a ship, and a steel beam fell off, missed his head, and landed on his foot. His foot was crushed. The first part of his testimony is that the doctors said that his foot would not heal and that there was a chance that even after surgery he might not ever walk again. Also, the doctor said that he could lose his foot. After the surgery, he was told not to put his foot down for anything.

One day he was challenged during a service, and when he was asked if he believed God's word of healing, by faith he said that he did. The Elder told him that if he really believed, he would put his crutches down and walk in faith. Although my dad heard the words of the doctor in his head, he exercised faith and put his crutches down and walked up one side near the pulpit and came dancing down the other! Praise God! This was the beginning of a flow of pure faith through our bloodline from his seed. Everyone in my family has the same opportunity—to receive this generational blessing of the gift of faith and blessings or to reject it.

After a couple of days, my father felt pain in his foot. He continued to stand on his healing, but after the pain became more intense, he went to the doctor. After they x-rayed his foot, they found out that the pin used to hold parts of his bone in place had to be removed. That area was completely healed, and the pin was causing the pain because it was no longer needed. His foot had been mended together internally by the hand of God!

My dad's entire life was one of faith. He just believed God because he knew what God had done for him. His foot healed wonderfully, and he became a living testament of God. But also through this situation surrounding his accident, he learned to increase in faith financially. He first learned to trust God through daily needs.

Immediately after the accident, my dad gave his life to the Lord. As a matter of fact, lying on the ground, he began to realize that if that steel beam had dropped slightly over, he would have been hit in the head, died, and been lost in eternal judgment. Needless to say, from that point on, he was eternally grateful and loved God with all his heart.

However, he was soon faced with other challenges. After accepting salvation, he became a faithful tither. He presented God with his firstfruits, the first 10 percent of any finances that he received. He had a wife and five children and was receiving only seventy dollars a week from disability, back in 1965. But out of those seventy dollars, he offered his firstfruits to God.

Yes, he would hear whisperers telling him that God would not expect him to do this now. He also heard the voice of the enemy saying, "How are you going to take care of your family on this? You can't afford to pay your tithes." My dad's response was, "I can't afford not to."

He continued to be faithful in giving, despite the battles. Sometimes he and my mom would not even know what we were going to eat for dinner. But when it was time to eat, God always provided. We always had good meals. As children, we never even realized that there was a financial issue.

We watched my father's life, and he was always blessed. He never knew which way the blessings would come, but he was just always blessed and favored by God. Throughout his senior years, my dad never wanted for anything. Growing up, we saw that his heart really believed that God would always bless his 90 percent as he planted a seed of 10 percent, and that was also a generational blessing that we believed and received.

Also, just like there are spiritual generational curses, there are spiritual generational blessings. I would hear my dad praying every single morning for all of us before he went to work. I wonder how many Christian children can say that they have heard their parents praying for or with them. Listening to him was my first experience of someone adoring and worshiping God from the heart. These were seeds of prayer and intercession being planted in my life.

Further, my nana was a prayer warrior. She, too, loved God! I remember one day after riding the bus home from her church, as she was putting the key in the lock, she lifted her hand and said, "I love You, Lord. Thank You, Jesus." I looked up at her, as a young girl, and I remember thinking, "Is it all that? Can't she wait until we get inside? Nobody can love that much!" After all, we were still in the hallway.

She was very much a lady. She was not loud or unseemly at all. But as a child, I remember thinking that we had just left church. Wasn't that enough praising until next time? But as an adult who has experienced my own challenges in life, I can say that I now understand my nana. When you travel through the streets and are allowed to get back home safely, you should be truly grateful for the protection of God. When just a small thought enters your mind on how great God is and how faithful He is, suddenly praise does spring up!

My nana would take me to noonday prayer when I was a little girl. I heard her praying, and I stayed there with her on my knees for as long as it took. It was supposed to be only an hour, but it seemed like an all-day event to me. But if this is what it took to be in my grandmother's presence, I decided that I could endure.

Who knew that all along my presence in the presence of God with those prayer warriors would plant everlasting seeds into my life? Who knew that later in life I would be called to war on behalf of others? Who knew that I would be called to be an intercessor? Who knew that God would use me to reveal warnings to those hearts that needed to hear? I certainly did not know. And there are powerful testimonies of victory because of the training that I received around the anointing. My family, friends, and I have benefited from this call, as well as countless others. And for that I am truly grateful.

Even when I look at mom and see how God has blessed, strengthened, and developed her since my grandmother and dad were called home to be with the Lord, I know that she, too, has accepted these generational blessings. As a matter of fact, as I look at my family, I can see generational blessings throughout. Through the prayers of those before us, the doors to generational blessings have been opened for us and our children and grandchildren to receive, as well as for future generations to receive. By my receiving these generational blessings, our lives and the lives of others have been saved, and for that we are grateful. Everyone in my family has the same opportunity to make the right choice.

You have the power and responsibility to teach those around you, to plant seeds into the lives of those around you, that they may embrace generational blessings. Give your loved ones something to aspire to. Show them victory and success. Show them faith and unconditional love. Jesus' purpose in coming, dying, and resurrecting is so that you could be free in every area of your life!

I have been through so many experiences in life that I never imagined that I would go through. Yet what has helped me survive and live is knowing that I have chosen to embrace generational blessings and the Word of God. Knowing Christ's purpose in coming and that there is purpose inside of me have strengthened me to not just survive, but to conquer. Finally, the Word and its power have liberated my mind and enabled me to stand beyond my ashes and to understand that I always have the power of choice. It all boils down to either a willingness to transition through to change, or a refusal to change and acceptance to remain ensnared in generational curses and end up as generations before you.

This chapter is entitled *"Escaping and Destroying Generational Curses"* because it denotes *a continual consciousness in knowing that anytime you open the door to generational curses, the enemy is just waiting to overtake you!* He is waiting for you to live under the bondage that he has used to enslave so many of your relatives. This is not to imply that you must walk around in fear, knowing that the enemy is lurking. However, it is to say that if you apply the teachings that God has for your life, through His Word you can live above any generational curse in your bloodline and walk in generational blessings, including the blessing of healing.

I understand that it sometimes feels like it takes more effort to live free from your yokes. But for anything that is worth having, you must work for it. Yes, Jesus did all the work on the cross; however, Satan will present you with anything that the flesh desires to keep you from working for what is of real consequential value.

The ultimate prize is liberation in your spirit, mind, and body. It is time to escape from any generational curse that may be holding you in bondage, and the way out is through Jesus Christ, who provides you with newness and destroys the curse from your bloodline. Renounce that addiction, fear, or sin. After you escape by being aware of the enemy's strategy and choosing not to accept the curse, then you must teach your family concerning any generational curses and blessings that is in your bloodline.

CHAPTER 12

The BREEDING GROUND OF A BLEEDING HEART

Throughout the ministry that God has called me to, oftentimes questions arise regarding relationship conflicts. Both men and women are hurting because of broken promises and shattered dreams. Once upon a time, you may have thought that you had met Mr. or Ms. Right. He or she seemed like they were sent special delivery just for you. Then one day you awakened and questioned why all that you had invested in this person seems to have yielded no return.

I believe that investments are important within a marriage relationship. I believe in marriage with all my heart. My parents were true examples of the God-defined marriage union. By pouring into their marriage throughout the years, my mom and dad received a magnanimous return on their investment. Yet I have also seen those who have sacrificed and invested endlessly and still found themselves heartbroken and disappointed. The question then arises whether they were investing in the right market; was this person the one they were purposed to marry? Or, were other factors to blame?

I have also seen those who testify of how they stood on faith, consulted God, and received confirmation that this was the one they were supposed to marry. Then, in difficult times during the relationship, they question if they really did hear from God or whether it was the dictates of their fleshly desires that provided a confirmation to marriage. If the answer is no, they did not hear from God, then this book provides several reasons why their marriage has not yielded positive return. If the answer is yes, they really received confirmation and acknowledgement through prayer and counseling that this person was the one, the question is now, "What happened?" Why are they not seeing their harvest?" Where is the return on the investment? Finally, you may wonder if there could be yet other answers to explore that contribute to the success or failure of relationships."

Singles

There are countless singles who are waiting to experience the joys of marriage. Some are frustrated and angry because it seems like they have been waiting and waiting, yet Mr. or Ms. Right never seems to manifest. As they get older, then they may experience the battle between the compromises of integrity versus the clock's endless ticking. Some people resolve this issue by bringing themselves to a place where they accept what their minds and emotions have grasped…that it was not meant for them to marry. They may deeply desire to wed, but they decide that they will settle for not ever being a candidate for marriage. And they try to accept the pain and disappointment that go along with it or deny the pain and disappointment altogether. Then there are those who actually have no desire at all to wed. They are comfortable in their decision and have just decided that it was never meant for them to marry.

Others may say that they never want to marry, when all along they really do. They are saying one thing yet yearning for something else. They believe that saying it will convince others that they do not want to marry and that they will no longer be faced with the age-old question "So when are you going to get married?" Still others continue to fantasize about the "chosen one," although their emotions tell them that desperate times call for desperate measures.

Singleness is a very important time in your life. It is a time to pursue your personal dreams and aspirations. It is a time to be made whole and deal with yourself so that when you get married, you will be an asset and not a liability to the union. Instead, some singles move from one broken relationship to another, only adding more and more baggage to their lives.

Singles, first you must understand that marriage failures are not because the Word has failed, but the failure is in human defiance to biblical principles. In marriage, you have two people coming together. You have two hearts and two minds becoming one. Therefore, in your single state, you should not only pray for a mate that God desires for you to have, but you should also watch in wisdom, as well.

In other words, do not let your heart blind you to obvious issues. Are you ever invited to be around his or her family and friends? Have you ever just stopped to observe his or her family? How does he or she interact with his or her family and friends? What are his or her friends like? What do you see? Do you see a family life, or do you see individuality within his or her family? In other words, if you marry this person, will your relationship grow closer, or through his or her individuality and segregation will your marriage consist of two people living separate lives? Do you see any generational curses running throughout his or her bloodline?

Remember, no one is perfect, and no family is perfect. We all have things to work on or towards. Every family line has its issues. However, you must consider that a reality could be that you may just have to deal with some of those curses down the road if your intended spouse has not rejected those generational curses from his or her life. And, you should never ignore obvious issues. Try to be sure that this is the person that was meant and sent to be in your life. Get confirmation from God! Your flesh cannot be your guide. Your heart cannot even be your guide, oftentimes. But, in my opinion, acknowledging God for His direction will give a sense of security down the road. Otherwise, if you go in on your own, you may be faced with issues that you were never intended to face and that you are not equipped to face later on.

If people grow up in certain types of environment, they may tend to adopt those things they have observed in their families or surroundings for years, whether consciously or subconsciously. If they come from a family that resolves issues by fighting, then that may be what they bring into marriage. If they come from a family that runs away and disappears or shuts down for days rather than confronting the issue, then they may bring this behavior into marriage. People do tend to mimic what they have seen before them and what they are most familiar with.

However, there are those who have seen the wrong choices before them, but they were determined to choose to go in the opposite direction. They made the conscious decision to choose a better direction for their lives. Is that the case for your intended? If he or she comes from a family that sits down to discuss problems and maintains a united front, then that may be the behavior that you will see within your prospective marriage. So it is important to spend time with your intended's family, if at all possible. Spiritual and social environments can tell a lot about a person.

Some people feel that you do not marry the family and would disagree with the prior statements. But I believe that the family line can be important. Certainly, there are those who are able to break away completely from destructive environments that they grew up in. I applaud anyone who has this determination and fortitude. With a made-up mind, a renewed mind, you can accomplish this for a better life.

Yet there are still some considerations to guide you. Consider what happens if a person was not taught responsibility within a marriage or has never known a true family relationship. You may go through an extended adjustment period with them after marriage, in order to gel and become one. Basically, all marriages have that initial adjustment period. This is natural. But some marriages will experience more turbulence than others if one or both partners are not willing to embrace family or marriage responsibilities. Do they (and you) understand how to move from single-mindedness to family consciousness? The values setforth in their perspective family lines may come into play. Sadly, you may never be able to experience a unified home if one or both are not willing to learn and grow both individually and collectively. Many marriages have succeeded despite turbulent adjustment periods. But that is because they both made a choice to work and invest in their relationship.

These points that are given are for you to make certain considerations before you decide to make a lifetime commitment. Consider what happens if your intended spouse has never mastered financial management. You may encounter financial issues that can be detrimental to your family and marriage. I encourage you, while in a single state, to attend financial management seminars. Attend marriage seminars, if you are contemplating marriage. Attend seminars on family issues that are taught by proven facilitators.

In your single state, it is important to discuss finances before marriage and to understand how your potential mate handles finances. It is recommended that you discuss and view your credit history and obligations in order to understand how bills are and should be handled. It is also a great idea to pay down or pay-off certain bills prior to marriage. When planning and merging incomes, each couple will need to do what is best for them. One person may be more efficient in one area than another. You must come up with a plan that suits your lifestyle, income, and goals regarding financial planning. Financial disagreements are one of the primary reasons for family disputes and often divorces.

You should also discuss goals, both individually and for the intended family. For instance, if a man, being the head of the family, does not have any goals or vision for himself, he will not generally have any for his family. Also, ask yourself how this man is perceived. Is he complacent? Do you see negligence? Or is he one who accomplishes what he reaches for? Does he understand family and financial priorities? Will he have a healthy balance between work and family? Sometimes people settle because they are so anxious to get married. But in the long run, communication, discussion, and understanding can save you a lot of headache and heartache.

As a single female, you should also have goals that incorporate future family, if you believe for a marriage relationship. What do you have to offer a man seeking a good wife? Are you financially sound or moving toward that direction? How is your credit? Will you be a blessing to this man or a liability? Will you help build his life or tear it down?

The Bible says that a wise woman builds her house, but a foolish one tears it down (Prov. 14:1). It is great to have a career, if that is what you two decide; however, no career is worth the severing of a marriage or neglect of your children. As a woman, if you do decide to have a career (and many today do including myself), you must prioritize and always remember that you also have a God-given gift to nourish your children and, as the helpmate, to invest in your spouse and marriage. Ambition is wonderful. I believe that a woman can be ambitious, intelligent, and a visionary. However, you will still need to work together with your spouse in order to understand priorities. Thankfully, today some roles may interchange to promote an efficient family unit.

Also, be sure to discuss children, prior to marriage. Does your intended spouse want children? Does he or she feel the same way that you feel about raising your children? Do you feel the same way about their spiritual upbringing? This is something that should not be taken lightly. Many women are fearful and reluctant to discuss things of this nature with the man they are prepared to commit to, because their priority is just getting a man. However, many of these same women are also full of regret later after they marry. If you really trust in God, believing that He wants what is best for you, then taking a little more time to delve into areas that will affect your future will be beneficial and not harmful.

When dating or when engaged, both of you are generally on your best behavior, and all looks wonderful. Promises are made because your focus is on that great day—your wedding day. The problem is that your intended mate has grabbed hold of those promises that you made throughout your dating and engagement experience. He or she is looking for everything to be warm and wonderful in marriage, and in the beginning, it generally is.

But what happens when the challenges of life begin to rise and affect the marriage? Proper decisions must be made in order to conquer those challenges. Unity must be exemplified. Resolution should not be based on the benefit of one person, but for the couple and the family. You cannot always accurately predict how your intended will react in different situations, especially if he or she has never before had to face the challenges of marriage or certain challenges of life. You cannot even really predict how you will react in some situations. Reality is the real test many times!

How decisions are made is extremely vital. This is why you must have the right seeds within your life (principles of God) that can spring up into a great harvest when you are confronted with vital decisions. To make the proper decision that could sway your relationship one direction or the other is a serious undertaking. But with wisdom, knowledge, compromise, and divine guidance, it can be done.

You definitely need God's help for that. During the challenges that you face, you will sometimes see another side of that person that you did not even know existed! This is often during the difficult times when it may seem like your back is against the wall. These times will help you understand your relationship in greater depth. Now you will gain a true and accurate picture of just what level your relationship is on, how you need to improve yourself, and what changes can be made in order for your marriage to be successful.

Singles please do not be so anxious for marriage that you settle in the process! First, invest the time and energy in yourself prior to marriage. Invest in being a healthy single, first. Invest in your wholeness, first. Then, as your mind turns toward marriage, invest in what you want to bring into the marriage to make it a wonderful and glorious experience.

Attend different venues of educational learning tools for enhancement to your individual life and later to marriage. Learn the spiritual foundational principles of marriage, family, and finance. The foundational principles do not automatically resolve every issue that you might face. However, having a foundational base does provide you with a strong structure to build upon.

Singles, please understand that there is an order in God. If your intended is not willing to submit to God, you should ask yourself if he or she will really submit to you and your needs. And finally, never marry with the intention of changing that person after the marriage. If there are serious issues or abuse prior to the marriage, they will generally intensify after the marriage.

Matters of the Heart

Furthermore, let us address the matters of the heart. Hurts and betrayals during any relationship can become a breeding ground for a bleeding heart. When you have experienced pain after trusting someone dear to your heart, you must make a conscious decision not to carry this pain. You must be willing to confront the issue, understand that it happened, and move on. Try to get an understanding of why it happened. Sometimes you will be successful, and other times you will not. But do not stay there in the pain and memory—move on!

This is not always easy. Emotional severing is one of the most devastatingly painful experiences to encounter. It is not like a physical wound that you can touch and salve. Instead, it involves the very deepest part of your being. You can watch a physical wound heal and know that it is healing. Soon the pain and discomfort are gone. But when you feel the sting of an emotional wound, the pain can seem eternal. You must understand that your soul has become tied to this person. And anytime there is a severing, cutting, or separation from the one that your heart holds, you will feel it.

Have you ever had a paper cut? Then you understand that no matter how small, because it has penetrated your protective layers, that cut is painful. Whenever you cut and penetrate the heart of a "soul mate," it is painful. I really find it so mind-boggling that oftentimes those who have themselves been hurt so deeply will find themselves being the ones who bring pain into the lives of those whom they say they love. This is a demonstration of the fact that this offender is not healed within him/herself.

Regardless of why you have experienced your pain, the key is to understand that if you choose to harbor the pain, it can eventually turn into resentment, bitterness, and even hatred. These feelings can be toward others or directed toward you. Carrying the pain will hinder you from being made whole, as well as hinder you from receiving God's best in a present or future relationship.

The heart is a very sensitive area. You should never make promises that you cannot keep or never intend to keep. You should also always be yourself and never present a portrayal of a fantasy character prior to marriage. That is because your intended will expect that fantasy at all times.

In dating, you should always be sensitive to the fact that a person's heart is a vulnerable place. It is not fair to another if you live in deception and play games that can cause a bleeding heart.

Deception is selfishness in action. Deceptive people are thinking only about themselves and their own desires.

When a heart bleeds, through it flows resentment, pain, anger, and mistrust. It also begins to form barriers, which can even keep out that man or woman who does embrace integrity, truth, and unconditional love. A bleeding heart is blinded by pain and cannot recognize a divine gift. This is one reason why men and women miss out on good relationships when they are presented. They are still hemorrhaging within themselves.

Also, as a single person, you must be aware that exercising wisdom in dating can keep you from experiencing unnecessary pain. Have your family, friends, church leader, or someone reliable meet your intended in early stages of the relationship. This is not to suggest that early on you will know that this person is "the one." But it will give that person a chance to interact with your family and friends...those closest to you.

Again, understand that not everyone who comes into your life is sent by God. You must not be so willing to give your heart to anyone and everyone. And you must not continually allow disappointment upon disappointment to compile and bury your emotions into a deep abyss. Then you become a cold and bitter person always living in the past.

You must also guard your heart at all costs. Guarding does not mean that you erect barriers, but it does mean that you are wise and cautious. Do not allow yourself to become another person who misses out on the blessings of God and special relationships because of your past pain.

Presentation and Perception

For her: Whether married or single, presentation and perception are important in their respective places. As a single, you must be careful of how you carry yourself. Your cover will be read. If you advertise practically every inch of your body with the clothes that you wear, then some men will approach you with interest in the outward package *only*. Ask yourself what image you portray. In order to attract the right person, you must portray the right image.

The point is that you carry yourself as a young lady in order to attract someone who is willing to treasure your virtue and value your worth.

In my grandmother's day, my mother's day, my day, and generations after me, a man is yet able to recognize a real young lady. He can sense a young lady by her walk and talk; by her grace, dignity, and self-respect; even by what she does not say or do. A *real gentleman* will recognize when someone is just playing the role of a young lady or actually lives that life. When it comes to getting married and having a marriage according to the Word of God, a real gentleman will choose a woman of integrity, honor and grace.

I realize that it is a different era now, but carrying yourself like a young lady is never out of style. A woman who lowers her standards is cheating herself. She will attract those of a lesser quality lifestyle and mind-set. If you lower your standards, then you must ask yourself, "Who and what am I trying to attract?" In my experience, those who lower their standards during their youth find that as they get older, they have to settle within relationships. Others end up never marrying. But they could have been women of virtue and integrity and been in place to receive the one that God had for them.

Certainly, you cannot expect God to give you His best when you have not given your best. God's best is the one that He has purposed for you in order for you to be a blessing to his life, in order for you to help him reach his purpose, in order for you to fulfill your purpose and in order for your children to be born into a family that will instill those things needed to launch them into purpose and abundance. Remember, your decisions are far reaching!

When you are presented each day to the world, how will you read? How do you look? Do you take the time to groom yourself? Do you come across as a bitter woman? Do you walk with a chip on your shoulders? Do you act like you are angry with the world? Or are you pleasant? Do you walk with confidence, or do you drag along with your head hung low? Do you follow the mass majority or are you a unique individual who stands true to personal convictions? If Mr. Right was sitting and watching you at work, church, a social function, or dinner, what would he see?

Now I realize that we all have different personalities; however, some things are just not good to carry or display. Some women will carry bitterness but turn it off temporarily to find favor in a man's eyes, and then after the relationship deepens, her real disposition comes out. Be who you really are, and yet still deal with your own baggage while in your single state. You need to deal with any baggage that you carry that would cause you to embody any negative and destructive attributes and chase away Mr. Right.

I am not suggesting that you turn into a little Ms. Sunshine who is in denial of her own true feelings. So please do not misunderstand. What I am saying is that being upset or angry at a situation is a human emotion. The Bible does say, *"Be ye angry, and sin not: let not the sun go down upon your wrath"* (Eph. 4:26). That means, do not allow time to cause you to carry anger, but attempt to work things out. Nevertheless, when a person carries any negative feelings for any length of time without ever dealing with them, they will fester and grow and contaminate her entire life. So I ask again, what does your life reflect? Will he like what he sees both inside and out.

For him: Men, remember that everything that glitters is not gold! So understand that you must be real with your feelings and intentions when looking for a wife. Otherwise, you may think what you have is gold, only to find out later that because you presented yourself as something that you are not, now you have nothing more than scrap metal. True integrity will seek true integrity.

Presenting yourself as someone who is loving and caring in order to gain a treasure, when your true intention is to merely conquer and possess the treasure for a fleeting moment, is deception. Some men want God's best and may come across to a young lady as God's best, but instead, it is only a temporary ruse in order to win her heart for his selfish gain. Be ready to commit when you chase after a young lady's heart. It is a dangerous game with terrible consequences when you have her heart in your hands, but you really do not care about her total well-being. You must really understand that there can be lasting scars when you damage someone's life simply because of your ego and nature to conquer.

To all of you who genuinely look for God's best, I assure you that He is ready to present her. Although, many men walk in dishonesty and deception, there are still many of you men who are truly filled with integrity. Do not let your future married life be filled with unbalance by marrying the wrong woman. Therefore, understand that the woman you marry can help build your life and be a great asset and blessing to you and your children, or she can tear it down. She can build your family or destroy it. She can cause every day to be filled with great regret. I ask you, where are you looking? Who are you looking for?

Also, if Ms. Right was sitting and watching you throughout the day, what would she see? Would she see control, arrogance, and pride? Would she see uncertainty, lack, or insensitivity? Or would she see a man who is strong and sensitive at the same time? Would she see someone who has reverence for God or someone who curses and blasphemes God? Would she see someone she can trust, or would she see deception? What image painted on the canvas of life would reflect you?

Marriage

Understand that marriages will be confronted with hurts and challenges at some point. Marriage is work and dedication. It takes time to cultivate and harvest. Loving seeds must be planted throughout. You must lend time in order to reap the harvest of your seed.

However, what happens when you have done all that you are required to do according to the Word of God and have yet to experience the harvest of return on your investment? Are you looking for harvest in a barren field? I believe that you must come to realize that even if you have sown into the right person, even if you have prayed and asked God if that is the mate for you, decisions made throughout a marriage are still a matter of choice. This is why you must continually pray for your mate and for yourself.

I am also a firm believer that if you do plant the right seeds, one way or another a great harvest will spring up in your life *if* you continue to seek God, trust God, and obey God, no matter what. *(This is to say that by obeying the principles of God, you are planting seeds into the kingdom of God, and no matter what, you will experience a great harvest. The harvest may not always come according to your expectations, but just understand that the harvest will come.)*

In marriage, you both may have dedicated your lives to the Lord; however, if one or both of you do not acknowledge the Lord in the decision making process throughout the marriage, then wrong decisions can occur. Decisions that can be an open door to separation (continuously living individual lives while still married) can occur. The door to confusion and dissension can be unlocked. The wrong decisions and actions can breed mistrust, whether financially or emotionally. It is vital to understand that success in a marriage is not a 100 percent guarantee simply because you both profess salvation. Rather, it is guaranteed when you both are standing and living on the principles of God according to His Word—when you have committed to do the right thing! Again, work, dedication, commitment and compromise all contribute to its success.

Wisdom in Covenant

In a marriage relationship, you must be careful not to grow apart. Years ago when I heard about those who left their spouse because they grew apart, I just could not understand it. I could not comprehend why a person would spend so many years with their mate and then one day leave after ten, twenty, thirty, or more years. But as I grew older, I began to understand that when one spouse no longer wants to invest in the marriage or in himself or herself, while the other still chooses to live life abundantly, one may not feel that there is any other option left but divorce. But, each one has a choice to compromise and come to mutual ground.

When interests change and one or both spouses are not willing to share in the other's interests, the relationship can grow apart. When you stop sharing new experiences together, you will grow apart. When intimacy, passion and sex are more of a distant memory than a treasured part of the relationship, you will grow apart. Recognize the warning signs! The sad thing is that with some of the marriages in which I saw these things happen, divorce did not have to take place. All it would have taken was compromise. Instead, one or both allowed selfishness to construct a large gap between them.

Sadly, many marriages that have ended in divorce have also left at least one spouse despondent because he or she never wanted the marriage to end. However, a successful marriage is based on the hearts and minds of two people. But when you have one or both parties unwilling to compromise, segregation occurs in the mind, emotions, and then physical being. When you have one or both parties living for him or herself, then you have nothing more than an environment of self-gratification. This is the complete opposite of how the Word defines marriage.

When you get so accustomed to not being willing to compromise or give, then you settle and just expect your mate to understand it. When you stop doing those things that attracted your mate and do not add any new favorable memories, then your marriage is in danger. You can get so absorbed in your own selfish desires that you forget to try to understand the needs of your mate. Or if you stop caring about yourself, you also, psychologically and emotionally, eventually check out of the marriage.

Furthermore, unresolved issues or embedded pain that has never been confronted can continually create barriers that soon turn your heart away from your spouse. You can live together and yet be an absentee husband or wife. Marriage should demonstrate unconditional love, relationship, friendship, and intimacy; it is the ultimate expression of oneness — spirit, soul, and body.

The Word of God talks about the foolish man who built his house upon sand. When the rain, flood, and wind came, it fell. But the wise man built his house upon rock. When the rain, flood, and wind came, his house was still able to stand (Matt. 7:24–27). The rock represents the principles of God. Marriage must be based on unconditional love, trust, honesty, integrity, and a strong spiritual base. When this is broken, there is a crack in the foundation and an imbalance in the structure that stands on the foundation. You want the foundation to remain strong and intact. Therefore, the truth of God's Word, integrity, respect, and unconditional love must be the basis that your marriage is built upon. This is the way that God intended.

The perfect example for marriage is the Word of God. The Bible says that man is the head of woman, as Christ is the head of the church. Christ loved the church so much that He gave His life for it. Then He told woman to submit to her own husband. Submission is a yielding, or surrendering and commitment. Most of the time, there is a negative connotation with this Scripture. But I believe that when a woman is blessed to be able to submit and commit her heart to the care, strength, integrity, spiritual fortitude, and love in the embodiment of a favored gift from God (that chosen man), then it is something that is not at all difficult to do.

What makes it difficult is when you are expected to submit to someone who does not have your best interest at heart, someone who is selfish instead of selfless or one who does not follow the divine plan of God. It is difficult to submit when that husband does not portray the love toward his wife that Christ did toward the church.

Christ's love was unconditional. His love was unselfish. His love was giving. It is easier to submit to someone who demonstrates unconditional love, a giving heart, and an unselfish heart. This does not mean that he is perfect, but that he is willing to be perfected. I believe that unconditional love is a love that develops into that unselfish heart. Your experiences and things you share, as well as commitment and growth process brings you to this type of love.

A wife knows if she really has her husband's heart or if it is divided. Also, it is difficult for a wife to submit to her husband if he has not taken his rightful place as the head of the wife (and family). Men, when you step out of your place as the head and relinquish your call as prophet, priest, and king of your home, then you create a terrible imbalance in your family. The foundation now has a crack. Then that woman will generally find herself taking up the slack in certain areas in order for the family to survive. Certainly, although submission is a command, in reality she may find it difficult to submit.

Husbands, you cannot pick up and put down your call. Rather, walk in your call as the head—her spiritual covering, her provider, her strength—and you will have her heart. This does not mean that you must be absolutely perfect. It does not mean that you will not make mistakes. However, it does mean that you have not given up on the investment that has been in your marriage. It does mean that you are willing to stay in place and be accountable for your wife and children and the call that God has placed upon your life.

Husbands please understand that when a wife sees you, she is supposed to see the image of God. Understand that when she sees that you are seeking God and that you hear from God, she is more apt to submit to your leadership. When you stay in the presence of God for leadership and guidance, she will see that you have been saturated in the glory of your Father.

Again, the Scripture regarding submission is a command to the wife; however, in keeping in touch with reality, many women will not be willing to submit to someone who consistently makes erroneous decisions through emotions, rather than receiving godly direction. If she sees that you are trying to grow, that you have a vision and plan for your life as well as for the family, then she is apt to submit to your leadership, with full respect.

Again - - I cannot say this enough - - husbands and wives need to understand that the scriptures instructing husbands to love their wives (Ephesians 5:25, Colossian 3:19) even as Christ loved the church and "wives, submit to your own husbands" (Ephesians 5:22, Colossians 3:18) are commands! Many times either the husband or wife will back away from the command to them when they do not see the results that they are looking for. The missing factor is accountability.

Even if your spouse is not doing his or her part, *you* be in place and do what is right. (This is not to advocate staying in an abusive relationship, but rather a strategy for basic marriage challenges). God sees what you are doing and will bless and honor you every time! Many times you may be too eager to reprimand or punish your spouse for what he or she is doing or not doing. You must understand that since your hands are in the situation, God has no room to work. Too many times, we try to do the job of the Holy Spirit. Therefore, God is unable to bring your spouse to accountability, because you have taken things into your own hands rather than trusting God. God will direct you as to how you should handle any given situation in order to benefit your family.

When there is an imbalance in the order of God, it is reflected throughout the marriage, resulting in mediocrity. This is certainly unfair, when one mate is looking for excellence according to the Word and the other settles for mediocrity. Christian marriages should be wonderful, above all! Notice, I did not say "perfect." You have two imperfect people coming together, so the marriage may not be perfect, as in flawless, but it can be wonderful and blessed.

However, there are believers who are facing the same challenges as non-believers and for the same reasons. Life has a way of bringing its share of problems. Certainly, this will happen. But it is how the difficulties are handled that makes the difference. If the difficulties are handled from worldly perspectives, then you are going to get the same results as the world. If you are a Christian spouse but behave like the world and live under its dictates, you will have the same results in your marriage as does the world.

Divine wisdom can help your marriage to be a success. There are marriages that looked like there was no other option but divorce. But through divine wisdom, God did touch hearts and minds and brought reconciliation. So no matter what your situation, always acknowledge God for direction.

Honorable Women

In Proverbs 31:10–31, the Bible speaks about the virtuous woman. This is the woman who works to be a blessing to her husband and children. This is the woman who meets the needs of her family. She makes sure that her family is presented in such a light that others admire them (although the admiration is not her goal, but love). Proverbs portrays a woman who loves her family and loves to lend her hand to whatever she can to benefit her husband and family.

It seems like we always hear about those women who are controlling, argumentative, or bitter, those who leave their children to raise themselves, but I would just like to applaud those virtuous, honorable women. There are many virtuous women who never receive the accolades that they are due. Sometimes they may never even hear a thank you from those they bless. Many are taken advantage of, even by their own families. But God sees everything that you do! He hears your prayers going up for your family as well as for others. He sees the sacrifices made for your family and how you have blessed others. So today I applaud you!

A virtuous woman will yet be in her place, no matter what. When she does this, then she understands that God still honors her and that accountability for her husband's role and actions is now between him and God. Now she is able to trust God, knowing that her family is in His hands!

In contrast, Proverbs 12:4 describes the characteristics opposite of a virtuous woman *(...but she that makes him ashamed is as rottenness in his bones - AMP)*. A woman can be a crown to her husband, as a virtuous woman, or she can be one who makes him and the household ashamed. A woman without wisdom is a woman who destroys rather than builds. Within us as women, we have the ability to build or destroy, to nurture or kill. A woman can be wicked and vindictive, or she can be loving and effective.

Women, remember that you will be effective in whatever you choose. Jezebel was effective (for a season) in choosing control, manipulation, evil, and murder. At the end, her actions brought death and curses to her and her house. Esther chose to use wisdom, to trust God, and to be effective. She was able to save a nation.

To be married to a woman who does not give and is selfish and unkind, despite a husband's will to love her as Christ loved the church, leaves a man challenged in his thinking and actions. But as long as he remains in the will of God, he will be blessed. She, on the other hand, is now accountable to God for her ungodly actions.

Women, to disregard your husband's *godly* leadership and to overrule his decisions with no real basis is to challenge and object to his divine position. It also causes you to walk in direct defiance to God. I am talking about a man who seeks after the heart of God. I am talking about a man whose life is based on the principles of God and who applies the principles of God. This is a man who looks out for his family, a man who provides and wants the best for his family. This is a man who seeks God to make the godly and wise decisions that will affect his family. A man like this is a prize in the sight of God!

For a wife to step out of place and walk in control, manipulation, and disrespect is unwise. To degrade her husband's character or his heart is foolish. Understand that a man's ego and self-esteem can deteriorate when he feels inadequate, disrespected or even feel that the essence of his manhood is threatened. I am referring to men who genuinely seek to improve their marriage and themselves. However, they may soon throw up their hands when a wife's harsh words and uncontrolled tongue are constantly berating rather than encouraging and uplifting.

A wise woman will see her husband through the eyes of God. She will understand that he is designed with purpose and greatness. She will try to understand that sometimes frailties or past failures can be used to launch him to success, rather than leave him sentenced to bondage because of failure. A wise woman will constantly pray and shower her husband with words and actions that yet make him feel like a man despite disappointments. If this man has unconditional love that is demonstrated toward you, he is a priceless blessing that must be treasured and reciprocated.

And if after all of this is done, if he is still not in place and lives against God's purpose and plan, let God be the one to move on your behalf. He is the one who sent His son so that *you* could have life and have it more abundantly. When you do all that you are supposed to do, then you have put accountability back on God. He now has to be accountable to His Word for your life. And I love it like that, because God's Word does not fail!

Distractions

Understand that there are too many distractions today that can sever your marriage. The Internet has provided such an avenue of deception and perversion. Countless people, including Christian men and women, have fallen prey to its susceptibility. Some will develop relationships in the online areas with so-called friends and then rarely chat with their spouses. Lives can be torn down through its clutches.

Yes, soul ties can develop through the Internet. When you are constantly hearing how wonderful you are on the Internet, yet your spouse is complaining because you do not spend time with him or her, take interest in the children, participate in family events, or wisely handle your finances, then, of course, your flesh will continuously draw you toward those enticing voices from the Internet chat rooms. You may want to hear how wonderful you are, but in the meantime, your home and family are falling apart.

What you try to deem as innocent soon becomes obsessive because of your need to escape reality. Undoubtedly, there are hidden issues that have never been dealt with if you are using the Internet to escape. Truthfully, if you come together with your spouse and family to try to resolve any issues in the home or in your personal life, then you can and really will be deemed as wonderful by those who matter.

Next, there are those who, regardless of how wonderful their marriages or families are, will still feel drawn to the Internet. Now I want to be careful and not throw complete blame on the Internet. It is a wonderful tool that has great and powerful information to benefit all areas of life. It is also a great ministry tool. However, when you have an issue already within, you can also be lured to the ugly parts of the Internet.

Even if you feel that you do not have any issues, you will be surprised what surfaces if you become involved in degrading areas of the Internet. Then your life becomes connected to others with issues. Anytime you have a relationship with people on the Internet that you call friends, yet your spouse and family are never introduced to them; when you never see them at a family, social, or church function but meet them on the Internet at the same time daily; when you receive their calls at work and receive text messages all times of the night; then that signifies that there is something unhealthy going on. This signifies that you have issues that you will not own up to.

This is just another strategy of the enemy to sever families, including Christian families! It has gotten so out of hand that universities, communities and even some employers have now formed counseling groups for those who are addicted to the Internet. Yet some people will always defend their side by justifying the fact that it is not like they are meeting outside the home, since they are still home while using the computer. But they are deceived to think that

a one-on-one meeting will never take place. If curiosity and enticement lures you into degrading areas or unhealthy chats, then it can
also lure you into one-on-one meetings.

Realize that each time these relationships develop through
deceptive and unhealthy means, seeds of segregation are being sown
within your marriage, as well as soul tie developments established
with those on the Internet. It is not fair to your loved ones who have
invested in your life. Despite the growing problem of Internet addiction, many ministries have not dealt with this issue. Thank God for
those who are addressing these issues, and it is my prayer that many
others will embrace this challenge to educate people on the dangers
of the lure through the Internet.

Through the deception that lurks through these areas of the
Internet, it has been a silent killer for some people. They think that
they can handle the lies, deception, and embracing of the enticing
words on the other side. Then one day they look around, and everything that they have worked for, invested in, and loved is gone.

Remember, anything good can be used for evil, especially when
money is involved. Sex is a lucrative industry. Sex does sell on the
Internet, as well as in the media. As long as this is the case, you will
always have those who use the Internet to entice while they make
money.

To spend countless hours away from your family on the computer
is not healthy. To have a secret life away from your family is asking
for trouble for you and your family. It denotes that there are issues
within that need to be dealt with. To have personal things locked
away from your spouse, such as a cell phone or computer (security codes), definitely raises suspicion, breeds mistrust, and can
demonstrates guilt. If there is nothing to hide, then this would not be
an issue. Yet, lust brings one to secrecy, lies and isolation through
deception.

The Internet does allow anonymity for ungodly activity through
multiple e-mails, X-rated sites, chat rooms, and microphones and
cameras; and it can feed the very inward desires of the flesh. But
it does not remind you that there is no anonymity with God! It can
make you feel invincible because you can present yourself as the
most wonderful person ever. Yet you do not realize the reality that

you are being held in captivity all while destroying your marriage and family.

Do not allow any tool that can be positive, such as the Internet, to be utilized in a negative way and lure you into the clutches of degradation or darkness. Be wise! (Re-read the section titled "Matters of the Heart" in this chapter as a reminder of the damage that you can do when you breed mistrust.),

Importance of Unity

During conflict, if you do not work *together,* it is like being stranded in the middle of the water and rowing at the same time in two different directions, even though both are looking for land. In relationships, it takes a willingness to push past you. All the decisions should not benefit one spouse. There should constantly be compromise throughout the marriage. (It is amazing to me when a Christian spouse finds that standing on the principles of God is a compromise to him or her. In other words, when you bring up a problem that conflicts with the Word of God and your spouse becomes frustrated because he or she will need to compromise personal desires in order to change, then carnality or selfishness may come into play).

One person should not be left to carry the weight of having a successful marriage. Both parties should be willing participants. Let us say that a couple decides to go to the beach or a resort and rent a two-seater bike. One is in the front peddling, and the other is in the rear. They are enjoying all the sights and having a great time.

Then the one in the rear decides to lift his or her feet from the pedals. This spouse decides that his or her spouse will not know the difference. He or she just wants to coast along. Then they are confronted by a slope, and one spouse is pedaling diligently while the other will still not help pedal. The spouse in the front is wondering why it is suddenly so difficult to move forward now. He or she is now feeling the weight of the situation while trying to reach the destination. The weight has shifted from a balanced situation to an imbalanced situation.

This resulted in one partner doing most or all the work while the other just coasted along and stopped contributing. This resulted in the other partner feeling the weight of the situation. This resulted in the severing of a team working together. One was pulling, and the other just went along for a free ride. Remember, the strategy of the enemy is always to divide and conquer. When both parties are not investing and pulling their weight, there will be an imbalance in the marriage, and the results could be the severing of a union.

Working together is the key to a successful relationship. Respect is vital to a relationship! When one person gives up and stops carrying his or her share, whether emotionally, financially, socially, intimately, or supportively, then you have an imbalanced relationship, which is an open door to the enemy. Too many soul ties have been formed outside of the home because an imbalance existed within the marriage.

I wish that there was a strategic screening team, as a rule for everyone before they wed. Oftentimes people wed and bring all their baggage to the marriage. They often bring unresolved issues to the marriage. They often bring past relationships into the marriage. They often bring selfishness into the marriage. Then the marriage does not last.

Also, longevity is wonderful; however, longevity without unselfish love and togetherness is still failure, in my opinion. God never intended for longevity and internal separation to be a defined image of marriage. Some people stay together for convenience or even because of fear, and yet they are miserable. They hide under the guise of marriage, but in fact, they live segregated and isolated (from each other) lives. This is all while the Bible is saying that God wants you to have abundant life! I believe that if you are together, the issue can be resolved if both are willing to submit themselves to biblical principles and compromise.

In marriage, there are significant changes and compromises. Sometimes change is essential in order for a relationship to be strengthened. Compromise is also vital in order for a relationship to mend and weld together. Please understand that effective communication is essential, because in various cases, the issue is not that you are not "doing," but that what you are doing is not what your spouse needs from you! Sometimes you may do or say what you think your mate needs and expects, but that may not be what your mate needs or what your mate desires. So communicate! Be willing to embrace change in order to improve your relationship, in order for your relationship to heal or grow. Sometimes change *is* necessary in order to go on.

Time to Change

Understand that each person has a free will. This means that you *are* capable of change. Some people are afraid of the word *change*. Some immediately begin to think about control, for instance, when they feel that they are confronted in certain areas. When a spouse addresses his/her mate and points out that change is needed in a particular area for positive gain, this observation may cause the spouse being confronted, to become defensive. The spouse being addressed may then immediately begin to go over his/her résumé and conclude that there is no need to change, by determining that there is nothing wrong with him/her. Hear what your spouse is saying!

Sometimes change is healthy. Let me be emphatically clear—indulgence in anything unhealthy and destructive requires an immediate change. So there is a major difference in needing a change to occur in order to benefit the marriage and family because of choices of destructive behavior versus change requests by a spouse simply because of his/her manipulation and control; that is to say, just wanting a person to change to suit ones personal selfishness.

Most of the time, the initial attitude taken when one mate requests change in order to benefit the relationship is that the other spouse is operating under manipulation, control, or has cloning in mind. But I find it unsettling that when the request is made for change, this stance is taken. Yet throughout the marriage, many times this same spouse being confronted has no doubt changed drastically (negatively) and turned into someone unrecognizable. As I speak with various people, one of the constant issues expressed is that the person they married has changed for the worse.

When you marry someone, you expect to experience life with this person. Change, as far as growth, is great. Change, as far as expansion, is absolutely wonderful. These types of changes will broaden your horizon and benefit you and your family.

Yet some people change selfishly and so drastically that it is as if you are now married to a stranger. Sometimes you may wonder if this is still the person that you married. Drastic change in a negative way destroys the marriage relationship because the one who has changed is now not the same person. I am not alluding to sickness, some tragedy, or a challenging situation. Every marriage will encounter challenges at one time or another. What I am referring to is selfish change that occurs when a mate is dealing with his or her own inner struggles, wants, and desires outside of marriage communication, team spirit, spiritual counseling, and biblical principles.

Or it can occur when that mate simply does not know how to handle the challenges of life. It can also occur when you become segregated and have all separate interests and activities apart from your mate. This is to name only a few reasons. So in marriage, you must be open to positive change that can benefit your relationship as a whole, as well as benefit the entire family.

Bleeding and Breeding

Whether a person is married or single, a broken relationship can, in general, breed resentment, hurt, abuse, anger, or mistrust. It can damage a person. It can destroy a person's self-esteem. It can ruin a person's faith in ever being in a positive relationship. It is a breeding ground for emotional anguish and permanent scars. But that is only if you choose to allow these emotions to become a permanent fortress of pain. If you choose to heal from them, then you can recover and move on.

If you have experienced a broken relationship, you may have attempted to try to understand what went wrong. But know that you cannot always understand, because you do not always anticipate the mind of another person. You will not always understand why the person did what he or she did or did not do. This is especially difficult when you feel that you have done all that you could to make things work. But this brings you to a place of accountability where *you* do not have to harbor hatred and bitterness, which destroys you. You can choose to move on and live!

Breeding denotes reproduction or birth. Breeding and birthing hatred, fear, or bitterness means that you begin to bring forth these same characteristics in other relationships that you encounter. If Mr. or Ms. Right is brought into your life, these same ill feelings that you choose to harbor can destroy that new relationship. These things can also filter into the relationships that you have with your children or others in your life.

Breeding is an extension of you. So if you have chosen to harbor bitterness and resentment, then your breeding is going to manifest in everything you touch, every situation that arises, and between those you have connections to. You have just empowered the perpetrator to continually bring you pain. You have just elected to empower the perpetrator to continue to enslave you each time you rehearse the issue that brought the pain, as well as continuously feed the pain through your own bitterness. Let it go! Forgive and move on! Only then will you be completely free to *live*. Do not let your heart become a breeding ground of mistrust and bitterness because someone has hurt you. Instead, walk in your empowerment and *live!*

Marriage and Ministry: The Ultimate Sacrifice

I believe marriage with ministry is a great sacrifice. Although you must be careful not to literally sacrifice your marriage, there is a definite change that occurs when one or both are called to ministry. To sacrifice is to give. You are not to give up your marriage, but instead, you are giving your time and sharing some aspects of personal life, as well as becoming dedicated to aspects of ministry. It can be glorious in that you work together, you join spiritual forces together, you walk in faith together, you grow together, and you experience the blessings and harvest together. Or it can be one of the most challenging experiences that you have ever encountered. The deciding factor is for both spouses to understand all that goes along with the call.

I am sure that if you are not new to ministry, you must now understand that your life, marriage, and family are put on open display through public ministry. People want to see the fruit of what you teach and say that you believe. People are also looking for lights.

Many will glean from other marriages after they see that the principles have been proven to really work—through yours!

Next, you must understand that you and your spouse are yet
individuals. This stands to reason whether either or both of you are
in ministry. You are still two separate individuals with your own
minds and emotions, yet you are united in marriage as one. If you
are conscious of this, then you can respect each other in such a way
that those who are watching you will be respectful of both of you.

There must not be any competition. You must be unified behind
closed doors and in the public. You must respect the gifts and
anointing that God has placed in each of your lives. You may have
to set issues aside to minister, but at the appropriate time, resolve
them. The moment you decide to live and display a segregated front,
you have opened the door to the enemy to continue to divide and
conquer. Many times those who have been watching you will allow
the enemy to use them to further burrow the pit of segregation.

It is important for you to understand your call as well as your
spouse's call (if you are both in ministry). If only one is in ministry,
it is still important to understand the call and all that goes along
with the call. This can make it easier to divert unnecessary conflict
down the road, whether internally (within your marriage or family)
or externally (from others).

It is difficult to move forward together when you are unbalanced. If one spouse is truly sincere in ministry, but the other is
strictly utilizing the position for entertainment and self-aggrandizement, this can pose a conflict. It is important to know that ministry
is a further call to servitude, not an opportunity for the flesh to be
glorified.

Ministry marriages can experience their share of conflict. If the
spouses are not wise, they can find themselves embattled in endless
emotional tug-of-war games. Understand that because you are a
ministry couple, many people may view you as celebrities rather
than men or women of God. Over the years, this attitude has not
declined, but sadly, rather grown. Therefore, there will always be
people who are trying to get close to you for the wrong reasons.
There are those who will try to play one spouse against the other.
There are those who despise the fact that you are in the position

that you are in and will do everything contrary to your ministry and marriage. There are others who will be envious of your marriage because you are in the place that you are in or because you have received the blessings or acknowledgments that you have received. They never consider the sacrifices and hard work. Some will even be envious that you are married to the person you are married to.

But it is up to both you and your spouse to always maintain a unified posture. It is also up to both of you to always remember that it is a blessing to give, and in ministry, you are the servant and not a celebrity. Yet it is equally important to remember that God never intended for you to sacrifice your marriage. In order to maintain a healthy balance, wisdom must be exercised.

Ministry Men, Beware!

One of the first calls to ministry for my life was to the areas of women and youth issues. When God calls you to something, He equips you thoroughly. I can tell you that not every woman who professes salvation, holds a position in the church, or even teaches the Word of God is of God. I am sure that this is no surprise to most of you, if you have been in ministry for some time. I am talking about deception under the guise of spirituality and religion.

As previously stated, women can build or destroy. They can be manipulating, controlling, seducing, and deceptive in order to gain a place in a man's heart. There are those who were married to these spirits before they accepted the Lord. Some were never delivered from these spirits. For others, when they first came to Christ, they pursued Him diligently until they were delivered. Then after time, some embraced these same spirits again and now operate in them right in the church arena. Some will minister out of their own seductions. They will use the pulpit as a place to control and manipulate, when all along, the root is that they have returned to their former lusts.

To my brothers, understand that God will not have you ignorant concerning the enemy's devices. Watch as well as pray! Do not be naïve in thinking that every sister in the church holds you, your wife, and your family with the best interest of heart.

In my experiences, I have seen women who cunningly win an open seat into the heart of a man, whether a brother, deacon, minister, elder, pastor, or bishop. They can sometimes portray their relationship as innocent on the outside, but all along, the relationship is used to satisfy their own lusts, rejection (from their own spouses or from their pasts), and seductive wiles.

I certainly hope that you are aware that temple prostitutes still exist. They exist in the form of seduction and manipulation in exchange for positions and titles. They exist in the form of satisfying such a woman's need for companionship with any man, regardless of whether he is married or single and whether she is married or single. They exist in the form of satisfying her need for the attention she craves.

I am not necessarily talking about a sexual relationship only (although that has been a factor in many cases). I am also talking about an emotional need to satisfy the inner craving for attention from the opposite sex. There are those who will even use other men as threats in the faces of their own husbands. This is, again, to control and manipulate their own spouse and to enjoy the deception of victory over another wife through the control and manipulation of that wife's spouse. Yet when this woman, operating under the dictates of Satan and the flesh, goes home and is left alone to reflect, she must still deal with her own loneliness, rejection, and insecurities. So again, let me reiterate, deception *first* deceives the one who has opened her heart to deceive others.

When I first thought that this book was completed, God placed it on my heart to go back and add this chapter. Through prayer and seeing the pain of some ministry brothers and sisters, I just wanted to allow God to use me to encourage you. You are in the forefront, and if the enemy can destroy you and your marriage and family, that is ammunition that he can use to destroy any of those watching.

You just do your part. You both have choices. You cannot make your spouse do anything. If you are doing all that you can according to the Word of God, you have a right to expect from God. Remember that God is the *final* authority; and if you believe that He has come so that you can have life more abundantly, then He will do all that needs to be done to ensure that this comes to pass for your life.

To prostitute is to *"devote to corrupt."* This means that a woman possessing this seducing spirit has devoted her mind, will, heart, and soul to corrupt anyone who is open to her lure. It means to have an *"unworthy* (shameful, degrading, dishonorable, disgraceful, contemptible, pitiful) *purpose."* Finally, it is to *"debase, destroy, lower,* or *degrade."* Not only does she debase her own self-worth by gaining a reputation in the church and living in deception at the same time, but she will debase the reputation of those whose hearts she penetrates. She will bring shame to her own husband (if she is married), her family, and herself. She will bring shame to any man who submits to her enticement, as well as to his wife and family (if he is married). Again, this is a lifestyle chosen by not only some single women, but also married ones.

Women of God, this is not to bring unwarranted suspicion to your sisters just because your spouse converses with the opposite sex. Let us have a mature mind. I am not teaching obsession, because in life and in church, you will have friends of the opposite sex. However, there is a way to go about this in wisdom and pure heart. And generally, there should be a fusion of friendships and relationships with both spouses when you get married. So, this is merely for both men and women to understand the devices of Satan.

Brothers, please understand that women can be so deceptive that they will stand in your presence and present themselves as the most honorable woman that you could imagine. Then they can work their way over to your wife and provoke her. Further, they will gloat in front of your wife, knowing that you do not even know who they really are.

I have talked with women who have had hateful and hurtful things said and done to them by other women—right in church. When I asked if they had mentioned it to their husbands—their praying husbands in ministry—some said that when they did, they were perceived as being paranoid, jealous, or as having misinterpreted this "honorable" (in appearance only) woman's statement or actions. This will ultimately bring division.

Brethren, communicate with your wife and reason through each situation. Come to a final conclusion. Remember, you are her spiritual covering. You two must decide if this person who has offended is someone that you want in your lives, and then you must handle the situation accordingly.

Now in addressing the fact that there are women who can tarnish your marriage, and yes, even right in the church, we must also address another side of the coin. These women are successful only because of men in the church who allow their marriages to be infiltrated. To both husbands and wives, never bring other people into your marriage! Decisions should be determined by the two of you. Men, your wife will recognize another woman's voice! This is, whether it is mom, sister or friend. So, come together and reason rather than turning outside for decision making.

Bringing up past relationships consistently as a way of manipulation is to build a wall that can stand forever. If you did not paint a clear picture of your single life prior to marriage, you certainly do not use it as ammunition after you are married.

Also, understand that you are drawn into temptation only to what *you* desire anyway. As I stated earlier in this book, there are natural desires, and then there are perverted desires. I am addressing perverted desires, which are desires outside the will of God. Whatever you are drawn to is that which speaks loudly to what is really inside your soulish area. It speaks volumes of your thoughts, emotions, will, and reasoning. Even in an innocent sense, it can place your life on a canvas and paint a picture of your true character and personality. Temptation is not a sin, but entertaining it and yielding is.

When there is an inconsistency somewhere in your spiritual life, oftentimes the thing or person that you are drawn to is not necessarily what you are outwardly promoting for your life. You say that you stand on the Word, but in reality, you may find it more and more difficult to do so because of your inconsistencies. The Bible says that *"but every man* [and woman] *is tempted when he is drawn away of his own lust, and enticed"* (James 1:14, emphasis added). You are drawn by that desire that has already been established in your heart. Only a renewing of the mind can change this.

Again, natural desire is not a sin. Yielding to a desire/temptation that takes you away from the will of God and purpose of God for your life is a sin. Yielding to a desire within the confines of the principles of God is a blessing. Whatever you carry in your life will eventually filter through your marriage. God does honor you for the stance that you take on behalf of your marriage. Therefore, as a brother, when you allow the voice of the temple prostitute to come into your marriage, when you allow her voice to come and influence your life, when you receive her as the third party to your marriage, then you must take inventory of yourself and look within. You must also understand that because of your choices, destructive consequences will inevitably follow.

Ministry Women, Beware!

Women, beware of wolves in sheep's clothing. Men who prey on vulnerable women will watch and observe you first before making their move. There are false leaders and men who prey on the distress and vulnerability of women both outside and within the church. Ministry women, your title does not exempt you from their clutches.

There are power pimps who use their titles or positions as a door of opportunity to manipulate, control, and conquer. There are some ministry men who pick and choose their ministry staff based on the satisfaction of their own fleshly desires, as if they were putting together a harem. There are those men in the church, whether ministry men or laity, who will study a woman to see how he can gain direct access to her heart. All along, his motives are impure. Women, single or married, *beware!*

Even if you are a ministry woman, it is easy to be deceived if there is something lacking within yourself or your marriage. Or it is easy to be deceived when you are dealing with natural desires, hopes, and dreams that have remained yet unfulfilled. If you are looking for validation or experience insecurities, it is easy for a predator to gain access, especially if he is operating under the guise of ministry, religion and or spirituality. As a woman, you need to be validated and confirmed at times. And just like it does with a man, the voice of flattery can cause you to make decisions based on your emotions rather than wisdom.

I have witnessed ministry women who pray and love God fall because of their hearts. The church has its share of power pimps.

These are those men who profess Christianity yet amuse themselves by collecting vulnerable women in the church. *(I just need to add that not all women who succumb to the wiles of such a perpetrator are always vulnerable. Sometimes they just make a willing and welcoming choice to submit to his enticement.)* These men are those who show no wisdom or respect when it comes to women. These are those who can appear to be genuinely caring and concerned, only to learn your weakness and seize sex and many times your heart, through your vulnerability.

This type of power pimp is one who can signal another woman to meet him in the hallway, although his wife is sitting right next to him. Yes, some of these men are married. Some are single. Some men do not move into sex, but their satisfaction is just to get close to you. But most of the time, these types of men do eventually look for sex.

To pimp is to dishonor for selfish gain. Thus a power pimp is one who is influential, notable through various titles, positions, or works, and who uses his position to entice and dishonor a woman for his own selfish gain. So, women, beware that this type of man can and will study your every move in order to find an opening to your heart. His heart is not toward you, but his desire is merely to seek you for selfish desires. This kind of man will use the power of his title, charm, or gift to meet your lack or to soothe your hurts or financial needs in order to conquer you. Also, I do not care how spiritual you think you are; if you do not bear in mind that there are those who prey on women, you can fall. None of us are exempt.

Understand that not all men in the church are power pimps. Some are just as vulnerable as the women. And, there are some women who just find themselves caught up in situations that they never intended to get caught up in, because they gave their heart to the wrong person. If you are married and find that you are constantly fantasizing about another man, if you find that the grass looks greener on the other side because of what you feel that you are missing in your marriage, then you can open yourself up to be enticed.

The enemy has a way of sending someone by who may also be facing issues within his marriage. Or it could be someone who is just dealing with his own hurts or insecurities. Then your mind may tell you that you are finally speaking with someone who can relate to how you feel. Realize that when you are most vulnerable, that is the time to surround yourself with those who can and will intercede for your life. That is the time to draw closer to God and not back up. But, the dilemma is when the flesh really does not want to be rescued.

We, as women, are generally sensitive and can find that lending our ear to someone else's hurts provokes compassion and sensitivity within us. But your compassion can lead you into a compromising position, if you are not wise. Do not even allow yourself to be found in compromising situations. Beware of the tactics of the enemy. We all must watch and pray!

A bleeding heart is a breeding ground for so many contaminants. These contaminants will poison your entire life. What flows from the heart will manifest in all areas of your life. Think before you act. Be sure to examine your heart before you make the choice and be sure to consider the purpose God has for your life and acknowledge Him in all things.

CHAPTER 13

STANDING IN AUTHORITY

Standing in authority is not a passive but an active posture taken against the enemy (Satan). It is a definite posture of opposition, both offensively and defensively. It is an out-and-out defiance against that which the enemy desires for your life. It is a definitive yes to God. It is an active position and outward demonstration of a surrendered will to almighty God. It is a willing heart, yielded in obedience to the will of God for your life.

To stand means to accept that whatever happens, God is in control. It is to believe beyond mere words, but with all your heart, that God is for you, with you, and working on your behalf. You believe that God knows and wants what is best for you and that if opposition, tests, or trials come your way, you can still come out victoriously.

Authority is the right and permission granted to you by God to operate and live above and beyond that which opposition perpetrates against your life. It is the ability and right to live above deceptive vices that may tempt you to choose the road to degradation and destruction. When authority is expressly used against the enemy, it brings you victory.

Authority is understanding your power through the Holy Spirit that moves on your behalf. It is the power of the Word of God that you speak, which causes both the angels and the Holy Spirit to recognize the banner that you live under and to move on your behalf. That banner is the blood (and the cross) of Jesus and your inheritance through His death, burial, and resurrection.

It is the level of authorization by God that enables you to rightfully posture yourself against the enemy. It is understanding that since God has authority, as His son or daughter created in His image, you also have power and authority to have a victorious life.

Some people totally misunderstand the meaning of having power and authority. They believe that if you merely speak the Word, you can cause situations to change on your behalf. There is more to it than that. First, understand that the authority is not you. The authority is God working for you, in you, and on behalf of you to glorify God. And it is understanding that when you stand under His umbrella, under His leadership, under His principles and purpose, you are covered by Him and therefore operate by His Word.

If a parent and child are together and it begins to rain heavily, if that child stays under the parent's umbrella, he will not get wet. However, the moment that the child steps out from underneath the umbrella, he will get wet, even drenched. If you step out from under the safety and covering of God, you will reap the consequences, and then lose the ability to operate in kingdom principles, as well as lose the benefits of the kingdom (of God).

Speaking the Word of God does not necessarily cause the Holy Spirit or angels to move on your behalf. They will move when they see the heart and life behind the words. Do not confuse this with those nonbelievers who seemingly prosper or even experience mercies. Some believe that just because they receive benefits in their lives, it justifies their sins.

God does love everyone. In Matthew 5:45, the Bible says that God causes the sun to rise on evil and good and that He rains on the unjust as well as the just. God loves and admonishes us to love everyone. But God's love does not mean that He overlooks sins. Make no mistake—sin is not overlooked.

But for some, prosperity manifests because there are also spiritual principles that are in this earth that do not change (reaping what is sown). If you work hard, you will see results, grow, and prosper. If you give, the seeds will come back to you. Some non-believers operate in their God-given creativity, talents, and abilities, which does yield favorable results. However, prosperity is more than just material blessings. It is wholeness—spirit, soul, and body. Material blessings cannot heal you. Material blessings cannot give you peace of mind or direction. Material blessings cannot make your life full of joy. It cannot put your family back together again. It cannot cause you to experience unconditional love. It can provide temporary happiness and pleasure, but materials blessings cannot save your soul. Therefore, you must put all things in perspective.

Sometimes God will bless or allow good things to take place in your life. Some blessings are simply the results of spiritual principles in operation; therefore, the consequences of the seeds that you have sown are manifested. Additionally, if there is a path of destruction that looks great, looks prosperous, makes you feel wonderful (for that moment), it does not mean that it is a door opened by God and that this is the divine will for your life. So let us not confuse all benefits and success in life with divine approval for a lifestyle contrary to the Word of God. The power that comes with authority is based on the heart and that alone.

Sometimes people speak the Word of God, and when it does not come to pass right away, they give up and make their own decisions. They do not want to wait for divine direction or guidance. Standing in authority means that you trust God and are willing to believe that His way is the best way.

Sometimes you may be faced with situations that seem so obvious for the right decisions: Should you move? Should you stay? Should you take that job that you badly need, although the hours contradict your service to God? But then, as you weigh the choices, pros and cons, it may become difficult, especially when there is a battle between the flesh and the spirit. In those times, just keep standing; keep trusting, until you receive the peace that you need in the decision. Standing in authority is saying that you will not be swayed by what you see or even how you feel. But you will wait until you have confirmation that the direction you need to take is in the will of God.

To stand in authority means that you understand your divine connection with God. It means that you acknowledge God as your commander in chief, as your Lord of Lords. I have heard people say,

"What would I need to pray over that for? It is a simple and obvious decision." But what they fail to remember is that many decisions have tentacles that reach to other areas. It affects their present and future. It affects other people in their lives. They do not know what is going to happen down the road.

You may not know the traps that await you. But God knows! If you do not receive direction from your leader, Father God, you may not know the destruction that awaits you down the road. So what may seem like a simple act of common sense can turn out to be an avalanche of problems if you do not trust God enough to seek His direction. This is why it is vital to stay connected to God and not wait until a 911 situation arises to try to connect with Him.

When you are encircled with despair, hurt, or frustration, knowing your authority in God brings you to a place of peace. It does not mean that the situation is automatically resolved, but it brings stamina in knowing that God is faithful concerning His promises. Standing in authority is an act of courage. I mean, to make a decision to trust God against all odds is very courageous.

Sometimes you may even feel silly during these times. No doubt, it did not seem logical to Moses to know that he was banished from Egypt but was told by God to then go back and face Pharaoh, with only a rod in his hand. But Moses obeyed God's instructions. When Moses had to approach Pharaoh with a rod and say, "Let my people go," he did not understand everything about God's instructions. He did not know what was going to happen next or how Pharaoh would react, but he obeyed God and the Israelites were freed.

When God told Gideon not to use the thirty thousand men to fight against their enemy but, in fact, to use three hundred men to stand against their enemies, Gideon was not sure what was going to happen. Gideon, like Moses, doubted his own ability to lead the people. He also did not feel equipped and certainly could not understand why God would tell him to use fewer men instead of more to stand against the army of Midianites. But Gideon obeyed and stood in place. When the Lord gave a divine strategy for them to divide and break the pitchers and blow the trumpets at the appointed time, the enemy became confused in battle and destroyed one another (Judg. 7:7-20).

When Jehoshaphat was given the strategy by God to put the praise and worship team in front of the military army (2 Chron. 20:18-24), it did not make sense. To us, it did not seem logical to place unarmed, militarily unskilled musicians and singers in the frontline of battle. But Jehoshaphat obeyed God, and saw victory!

So many people miss out on the extraordinary because they will not step out and allow God to also be their Lord. This is why many professing believers continue to experience religion rather than know relationship. They simply continue to embrace mediocrity. The flesh values comfort. To trust God and stand in authority does not always feel comfortable. Sometimes it causes you to stand out like a sore thumb. Sometimes it leaves you standing alone for a while. But at the end, you are redeemed by the victory that God brings into your life!

Always remember, the foundation to victory is obedience to God. God is a God of strategy and order. You may not understand everything that you are instructed to do, but obey His voice! We make decisions based on our needs, our desires, and our comfort, but God instructs based on the strategic plan for our lives.

This is why it is important to renew your mind in the Word. Your soul feeds on comfort. It feeds on stability and what it is familiar with. It ties you to your past issues, past feelings, and past experiences. This is why it is vital to renew your mind.

Renewing gives you a new perspective and thought life, which enables you to trust God through His promises in the Word. Hebrews 4:12 (AMP) says, *"For the Word that God speaks is alive and full of power [making it active, operative, energizing, and effective]; it is sharper than any two-edged sword, penetrating to the dividing line of the breath of life (soul) and [the immortal] spirit, and of joints and marrow [of the deepest parts of our nature], exposing and sifting and analyzing and judging the very thoughts and purposes of the heart."*

The Word of God is the only thing that can penetrate your soul (mind, intellect, reasoning, emotions, will) and delve into the deepest parts of your being. The Word of God uncovers and exposes you! Understand that God is the supreme physician. He uncovers and opens you up to expose the infectious disease that has infiltrated your life and so that He can bring healing.

Sin or negative habits and vices become such vital parts of your soul that abiding in them becomes so natural to you. This is why some can see chaos and confusion in their lives but will not take steps to rise up from the pit. Some people become comfortable in the pit. Their mind, intellect, reasoning, emotions, and will have indulged in destructive behavior for so long that to not live in chaos and confusion becomes uncomfortable, fearful, and frustrating. Why is it that some prisoners who have served time can come out and live in freedom but end up back in prison within a short time? It is because their soul (mind) has become accustomed to an imprisoned environment, and the soul dictates to them that it does not want to know any other way.

Even when your spirit man is surrendered to God, your soul still has to be renewed in the Word in order for your life to actually see change. Many try to change in their own strength. They will stop doing this or that because they were told that it was wrong. And this is fine. However, for permanent and lasting change, understanding why an act is wrong or destructive to you will benefit even more. Understanding the plan and strategy of God for your life will benefit you even more. Understanding that you were created with purpose will benefit you even more. Understanding God's love and promises for you has greater weight than just ceasing from participating in destructive behavior only because someone tells you to. All of this comes from understanding the Word of God. The Word puts the soul and spiritual aspect of your life in perspective according to God's perfect plan for you!

God has blessed each and every one of us with gifts, talents, and abilities, all for His purpose. But many of you are still waiting. What are you waiting for? Some of you have received prophetic words over your life, as well as promises, but you have never stepped into them.

"For as the body without the spirit is dead, so faith without works is dead also" (James 2:26). This Scripture is powerful! You have, no doubt, attended a funeral before. After you view the body, it is amazing to know that the person used to be full of such life. It

is often hard to believe that you are looking at that same person you were so familiar with, who is now dead. This person's spirit and soul are gone.

The Word of God says that *"faith without works is dead"* (James 2:20). This means that you can confess that you have faith all that you want, but if you do not walk in it and work it, then your faith is dead. You will not see results. So many people talk faith, but as soon as trouble comes, they run in the opposite direction. They change their stance. They go back to that which they left, because it is more familiar.

Also, understand that all of us have been granted a measure of faith. Your life operates in faith daily. However, where you place your faith is the key. Is your faith directed toward God and His will for your life, or is it directed toward your general senses and intellect?

Many trust in the practical things of life that are seen, such as careers, finances, or family, over the Word of God. So as you can see, life generally causes you to exercise some aspect of faith daily. When you go to work, you have faith to believe that you will be paid for the work that you have done. When you go to the doctor, you have faith to believe that he or she will diagnose you properly and prescribe the right remedy for your ailment. When you leave your family in the morning, you generally do not even think about whether you will see them again at the end of the day. It is just assumed and believed that you will. So, practical aspects of life do cause you to exercise some aspect of faith.

Remember the children of Israel? After God freed them from Pharaoh and they were in the wilderness, when it looked like their backs were against the wall, they began to murmur and complain. At that point, they even determined that they would rather go back into Egypt and suffer persecution than trust what they could not see (Ex. 14:12). This was a true demonstration of letting go of faith.

They had prayed and prayed for years for deliverance, but rather than continuing to trust God, who had delivered them from Egypt and fed them in the wilderness, their souls began to yearn for familiarity, even coupled with abuse, in order to know where their next meal was coming from. They wanted the convenience.

God had already done so much for them. They could have remembered that despite the hard taskmasters, God had caused them to multiply and grow. (And even in your hard situations, God can cause you to multiply and grow.) But their souls began crying out for their past. This is exactly what happens to many people when challenges get too hard. They begin searching for their own way out instead of continuing to trust God and His will, which is the best that He has for them.

Putting faith into action means that you do not just sit and wait. Now there are times when God will specifically instruct you to stand still. In those times, that is exactly what you do! You are waiting in faith. But in other situations, you must put faith in motion by taking action. If you need a job, you will not just sit and wait. You will put a résumé together. You will complete applications. If you need additional training, you will complete various training courses by going back to school. Some jobs even offer special training for advancement. All these steps taken are steps of faith, believing that these acts will help you land a job.

There are a myriad of testimonies in which God even blessed people with positions and careers that they were not even qualified for. Their faith enabled God to work outside of their limitations. They believed and expected God to provide.

Another case in point is one in which someone is praying for a spouse. What environment do you find yourself in? Is the environment conducive to the type of spouse you want...the one that God has for you? There are professing women who desire to wed. Yet they will take a chance in going to the bar to look for Mr. Right and then believe that they will save him or change him later on after they are married. If you choose to live for God, then you should want your spouse to do the same. Walking outside of His will for your life is not walking in faith.

There are women and men who have been praying for a mate. Yet they bury themselves in the house. They never attend fellowship, recreational, social, community, or family activities. Instead, they stay home, and then they want to know why the right one has not come into their lives. They are not putting faith into action.

Faith is knowing that as you are living (which does entail fellowship, positive activities and events, recreational events, and educational learning, for example), then the one God has for you will see you diligently working and living and will be brought into your life. Even being in the right career, the right job at the right time, can order your steps to your mate. This is why acknowledging the Lord in all things is important. After acknowledging, walk in faith. You must always have a balance in your life! Having a balance includes both faith and works. Faith without works is dead. You can miss out on God's blessings when there is an imbalance in your life. Faith is action through the revelation of the Word.

Again, Deuteronomy 30:19 says, *"I call heaven and earth to record this day against you, that I have set before you life and death, blessing and cursing: therefore choose life, that both thou and thy seed may live."* God has placed spiritual principles in place on this earth for your benefit. He has provided you with spiritual authority through Jesus Christ. He has equipped you to be victorious with the tools of His Word, in which there is great power. He has gifted you with a measure of faith that can be increased greatly as you put it to use.

God has spoken countless blessings over your life. He has empowered you for purpose according to His divine plan. He sent His Son, Jesus Christ, so that you could have abundant life. He has established eternal protection for you from the enemy. All excuses have been destroyed, because for every excuse, the Word of God penetrates and destroys the lie from Satan and prevails in truth.

What He wants to do for you, He has already done for so many others. The final choice is *YOURS!* Walk in the power and authority that you have been given! *THIS DAY* stands before you: life and death, blessing and cursing. You have the power and gift of choice. Now the rest is up to you! Make this your declaration and testimony: "Out of my ashes, I WILL RISE!" This day, choose life!

CHAPTER 14

IT'S TIME TO RISE!
Taking Back My Life

This chapter is an interactive exercise to motivate you to move forward from where you are. I believe that it is important to set goals. I believe it is important to establish written goals that you can often refer to. These goals should be posted someplace where you can see them every day.

I remember years ago when the idea of writing my goals appealed to me. It was during a time when I was going through so many transitions in my life. But I took the time to write down my goals and desires. At that time, many seemed far out of my reach. Yet I knew that with work, faith and dedication, they were obtainable.

On my list, there was no particular format. I just wrote down those goals that I could reach for over the next couple of months and years. However, over the years, I have learned to establish *immediate goals* (1 month to one year), *short-term goals* (one to four years) and *long-term goals* (five or more years). When I make an entry, I put the date that I begin working toward that goal, and then I list the goal. After completing the goal, I check it off.

Your goals should answer the following questions:

➢ Where do I want to go from here? (*Examine where you see yourself one, three, five, ten years from now.*)

➢ What are the practical aspects of my goals? *(You must be sure to set realistic goals that can be measured and attained. Remember that a desire is not necessarily a goal. A goal is something that you can attain through work and commitment.)*

➢ What steps do I need to take in order to achieve this goal? *(Think about each step that you will need to take in order to reach your goal.)*

➢ How do I take these steps toward my goal? *(You may need to do research on the Internet, in the library, through books, or via other resources. You might also consider speaking to someone who has already achieved this goal.)*

➢ Why do I want to obtain this goal? *(Is this goal something that is going to bring about a positive change in your life? Does it bring immediate or long-term gratification? Was it birthed in your heart, or did you randomly decide on this goal because you heard that it was someone else's goal?)*

Remember, this is just a basic recommendation. You can edit accordingly. After your goals are determined, you will need to outline and track them. This will allow you to do the following:

➢ Assume responsibility for reaching your goals
➢ Stay focused
➢ Measure your accomplishments
➢ Determine if you need to add additional steps or do further research
➢ Mark off each goal as you accomplish it

Do not be discouraged if you fall behind the deadline that you set for some of your goals. Just continue to be motivated. Your goals can be a compilation of personal growth or development, health and fitness, spiritual, relationship, recreational, financial, educational, career, or other goals.

This is just a strategy that I am recommending because it has worked for me. I had a list of goals that I posted on the door of my closet years ago. Every day I had to look at that list, and one by one, each goal was met. This was over a few years, but all the goals were met! I asked God for direction and wisdom and was able to meet those goals. This exercise is still a part of my life.

The best way to start working on a goal is to gather as much information on the subject as possible. If one of your goals is financial, then you should begin by attending basic financial seminars or purchasing books that will provide you with knowledge for financial stability and development. If one of your goals is educational, then you should look for classes that can offer you the accreditation that you need. If there is the issue of cost, you will need to review the scholarship, grant, and/or loan requirements. You can speak with the financial department at the school that you desire to attend. Also, you can check with your job or with religious or social organizations to see if they have programs that they offer for educational growth. If you check the Internet, you may be able to find alternative learning resources. Basically, what I am trying to say is that you always have to take the first step. Take the initiative to gather the information, and stay committed. Sometimes it may seem like you are at a dead end, but one more step can mean the difference between staying where you are and change. Do not always wait for opportunities to come to you; there are times when you must take steps to make opportunities happen for you. Be persistent in your thinking and determination. You must work for your success. Remember, "no pain, no gain."

There are so many obstacles that can envelop you as you try to move forward. So to summarize each scenario is just not plausible. Some of you may be faced with the ashes of a problem marriage or a divorce. Others of you may face the ashes of loss of employment or loss of a loved one. The issues are just so vast.

Nevertheless, if you understand the basics outlined in this book, you will be able to move on from where you are. Spiritual principles have been outlined throughout this book, but there are also practical applications that can determine your success or failure. Educate yourself. Surround yourself with people who are positive and who can impart positive seeds into your life. Some of you may need to change your friends if you want to make positive changes in your life. Others will just need to adjust from within.

Here are some other questions that you should ask yourself:

> Am I in a healthy spiritual environment that provides the true Word of God?
> Do I have a *positive* support system (family, friends)?
> Do I fellowship with any group that offers positive growth and development (community, social, spiritual)?
> Does my church offer counseling for my situation?
> Do the people in my life build my life or tear it down?
> Am I living in conjunction with God's purpose for my life?
> Do I know and understand God's purpose for my life?
> What changes do I need to make in my life in order to rise out of these ashes?
> Am I really willing to change?
> What decisions have I made in the past that brought me to ashes?
> What have I learned from these decisions?

Spiritual Breakthrough (Healing and Deliverance)

For those of you who are reaching out for help in areas such as addiction, emotional or psychological healing, there are certain steps that I recommend. I would first recommend praying and asking God for His forgiveness and to receive His Son, Jesus Christ, as your personal Savior. Then I recommend praying and asking God to lead you to a Spirit-filled church. This is a church that teaches the complete Word of God.

I also recommend seeking counseling. While searching for that Spirit-filled church, also ask them what types of counseling programs they offer. I believe that if the foundation of your life is a spiritual base, then the other aspects of your life will align. Your immediate goal is to be supported in prayer, enveloped by those who will speak life to you and counsel in your area of need in order for those strongholds to be broken and destroyed off your life.

Additionally, your local community should have resources that you can access for your individual needs. If you are looking for employment, there should be local employment agencies that can recommend training programs or provide you with job listings. Another viable resource would be your local crisis center.

Oftentimes, even hospitals can provide information on the various types of programs that they offer to the community. Furthermore, various honorable television ministries have prayer lines, or crisis lines, that can provide you with needed information. If you are blessed to have believers in your family, you may want to reach out to them in your time of need as a source of support. They may also be able to provide vital recommendations to you for your situation.

Your daily walk should include the following:

- ➤ *Prayer* for God to lead you to the right people and places.
- ➤ *Reading* God's Word and *studying* God's Word. Study until you receive enlightenment and understanding of the text. You may also need to purchase a concordance and commentary if you do not have one.
- ➤ *Daily confessions* of the Word for your life. Stand on the promises of the Word for your life. Reach for the Word when challenged by life.
- ➤ *Praise* God for what He has done for you already. Praise God for what He is going to do for you. *Worship* God for being the wonderful Father He is and the final and ultimate authority for your life.
- ➤ *Giving.* Give to others by reaching out and meeting a need. Whether it is giving advice, lending an ear, providing encouragement, meeting someone else's financial need, or extending your life to help another, just let the love of God be demonstrated through your life; give and you will be blessed.

After your healing process has begun, then you are able to be more focused on setting and attaining goals. All it takes is a willing heart and mind to rise out of some pits. For others, it takes a mind to persevere and contend for the promise. Spiritual warfare, faith, and the power of the Word is what you will need as weapons to prevail against the strategies of the enemy. Remember, we know the end results according to the Word. You are a winner! Rise up and live, in Jesus' name!

SAMPLE GOAL CHART

(This is a basic format. You can also add a column for the date initiated. You may also add or edit according to your personal preferences.)

IMMEDI-ATE GOALS (1 month–1 year)	Completed √	SHORT-TERM GOALS (1–4 years)	Completed √	LONG-TERM GOALS (5+ years)	Completed √

BIBLIOGRAPHY

Passer, Michael W., Ronald E. Smith. <u>Psychology: The Science of Mind and Behavior</u>. New York: McGraw-Hill, 2004. (Includes Psyk.trek™ 2.0)

Vine, W.E.; Unger, Merrill F., White, William Jr., ed., <u>Vine's Complete Expository Dictionary of Old and New Testament Words</u>. Nashville, Tennessee: Thomas Nelson, Inc., 1996.

Root, Orrin, Eleanor Daniel. <u>Training for Service</u>. Cincinnati Ohio: Standard Publishing, 1983.

<u>The Merriam-Webster Dictionary</u>. Based on Merriam-Webster's Collegiate® Dictionary, Eleventh Edition, Springfield, Massachusetts: Merriam-Webster, Incorporated, 2005.

CONTACT INFORMATION
W. D. Kidd Ministries
208 Eagle Valley Mall, #390
East Stroudsburg, PA 18301
E-Mail: wdkiddministries@yahoo.com

LaVergne, TN USA
30 September 2009
159534LV00002B/10/P

9 781607 916925